I Ching

I Ching

he Ancient Chinese Book of Changes

CHARTWELL
BOOKS, INC.

Introduction

The I Ching (also known as the Book of Changes) is one of the oldest and most respected oracles in the world. In its present form it can be traced back three thousand years, and even then it was old, being based on more primitive oracles. It has survived intact through the centuries because wise men in every age have held it in high esteem as a source of profound wisdom and valuable guidance, both in the search for spiritual enlightenment and in the conduct of material affairs. Its elusive magic has captivated some of the greatest minds the world has known, from that corner-stone of traditional Chinese society, Confucius, down to C. G. Jung. Today it is probably more widely known and more frequently consulted by people in all walks of life than at any previous time.

The I Ching is constructed around 64 six-line figures whose English name is hexagrams. These are made up of all the possible permutations of a broken line and an unbroken line in combinations of six. All phenomena are the result of the interaction between positive, creative, masculine yang forces, and negative, passive, feminine yin forces. Yang is represented by the unbroken lines and yin by the broken lines which go to make up each hexagram. In this way the 64 hexagrams can be said between them to symbolise all the stages of change and flux operating in the universe, and the texts of the I Ching describe these changes and apply them to the preoccupations of mankind.

The hexagrams on the following on pages are each accompanied by several texts. The first text, called The Judgment, is the oldest. It was composed by King Wen, founder of the Chou dynasty, after he had been imprisoned by the last Shang Emperor, Chou Hsin. The second text, the Commentary, is one of the later interpretations attributed to Confucius, though he is unlikely to have written it himself. The third text, The Image, is another Confucian commentary. It is intended to explain how the sensible person who follows the I Ching's advice – generally referred to as the 'superior man' – would act at such a time. The final group of texts, one attributed to each of the six lines of the hexagram, were composed by King Wen's son, the Duke of Chou, who destroyed the Shang dynasty in 1027 BC. These short and often enigmatic lines were written about forty years after King Wen's text.

To each of these groups of texts, the author has appended some explanation.

I Ching Book of Changes *Simplified Han*

易經

Traditional Han

How to consult the I Ching

The I Ching can be consulted in three ways. The first involves the use of a bundle of 50 sticks, the second requires three coins, and the third uses six specially marked wands. Of these methods, the oldest and most venerated is the 50 sticks technique.

The 50 Sticks Method

You need 50 narrow, wooden sticks, each about a foot long. Traditionally these are dried yarrow stalks, but pieces of bamboo will do.

Your copy of the I Ching should be kept on a shelf fairly high above the floor, and wrapped in a clean piece of cloth, preferably silk. When you consult the book, it should be placed on a clear table and unwrapped, the book lying on the silk. The sticks should be kept in a simple box on the same shelf.

In ancient China, the seat of wisdom and judgment lay in the north and those giving audience always faced south. You should place your table in the northern part of the room and approach it from the south. Lay the sticks in front of the book and light a small incense burner beside them.

Before consulting the I Ching, you should make three kowtows to the floor and, while kneeling, pass the 50 sticks three times through the incense smoke.

Compose in your mind the question you want to put to the oracle. Remember that the I Ching does not tell the future, but offers advice on how to act in the present to make the best of the future.

1. Take one of the 50 sticks and put it aside. It will not be used again but is included in the bundle to make up the significant number 50.
2. Using your right hand, divide the sticks into two heaps.
3. Take one stick from the heap on your right and place it between the ring finger and little finger of your left hand.
4. Remove sticks four at a time from the heap on your left until there are four or less left. Place these remaining sticks between the left hand middle finger and ring finger.
5. Remove sticks four at a time from the heap on your right until there are four or less left. Place these remaining sticks between the index finger and middle finger.

You will now find that the sticks held between the fingers of your left hand total either 5 or 9 (1 + 1 + 3, 1 + 3 + 1, 1 + 2 + 2, or 1 + 4 + 4). Put these sticks to one side.

Gather together all the discarded sticks (totalling 49 minus the 5 or 9 you have just laid aside) and work through the process of dividing again, starting with stage 2.

When you have done this you will find a total of either 4 or 8 sticks between the fingers of your left hand (1 + 1 + 2, 1 + 2 + 1, 1 + 4 + 3, or 1 + 3 + 4). Put these sticks aside.

Gather the discarded sticks together once more, omitting the two small heaps of 5 or 9 sticks and 4 or 8 sticks. Now divide the sticks a third time, starting with stage 2.

At the end of all this you will have, in addition to the discarded sticks, three small heaps. The first will contain 5 or 9 sticks; the second 4 or 8 sticks, and the third also 4 or 8 sticks. Look up the three numbers you have:

5 + 4 + 4	▬o▬	Old Yang line
9 + 8 + 8	▬x▬	Old Yin line
5 + 8 + 8	▬▬▬	Young Yang line
9 + 8 + 4	▬▬▬	Young Yang line
9 + 4 + 8	▬▬▬	Young Yang line
5 + 4 + 8	▬ ▬	Young Yin line
5 + 8 + 4	▬ ▬	Young Yin line
9 + 4 + 4	▬ ▬	Young Yin line

The line that corresponds to your three numbers is the bottom line of your hexagram. Note it down. To arrive at the second line up from the bottom you must gather together your 49 sticks and once more work through the stages of dividing and counting.

This must be done a further four times to arrive at the six lines of a complete hexagram.

If your hexagram is made up of just Young Yin ▬ ▬ and Young Yang ▬▬▬ lines, read the hexagram's Judgment, Commentary, and Image. Ignore the Lines, which are not appropriate. But if your hexagram contains one or more Old Yin ▬x▬ or Old Yang ▬o▬ lines, read the Judgment, Commentary, and Image, followed by the Lines.

Each of the four types of line is given a 'Ritual Number' from 6 to 9:

- ▬▬x▬▬ 6
- ▬▬▬▬▬ 7
- ▬▬ ▬▬ 8
- ▬▬o▬▬ 9

This is why the passage referring to each of the six lines of a hexagram begins **'In the third line, SIX...'**, or **'In the fifth line, NINE...'**. Six and Nine are the Ritual Numbers of Old Yin and Old Yang lines.

If your hexagram has one or more of these significant lines, you can take your consultation a stage further. The old lines are also known as moving lines, because they are thought to be in a state of change and about to become their opposites. An Old Yin line can be changed into a Young Yang line, and an Old Yang line can be changed into a Young Yin line, giving you a second hexagram. Read the Judgment, Commentary, and Image of this hexagram and it will throw extra light on your original question.

The Three Coins Method

This is a quicker but shallower technique. In this method, the toss of three coins gives us the lines of the hexagram. As with the yarrow stalks, the first toss gives the bottom line, and so on upward. On Chinese coins, the inscribed side is given a value of 2, the blank side 3. If you use western coins, 'heads' is valued at 3, 'tails' at 2. So a toss of three coins can give you totals of 6, 7, 8 or 9, indicating respectively Old Yin, Young Yang, Young Yin, and Old Yang.

The Six Wands Method

You need a set of six wands about 8 inches (200mm) long, 1 inch (25mm) wide, and ⅛ inch (3mm) thick. Each wand should be coloured black on one side and on the other side black with a 1½ inch band of white across the middle.

When a wand falls with the all-black side up, this counts as an unbroken, yang line ▬▬▬▬. When a wand falls with the white stripe up, this counts as a broken, yin line ▬▬ ▬▬.

Shuffle the six wands behind your back while concentrating on your question and roll them onto a table in front of you.

Straighten them into the form of a hexagram, starting with the wand closest to you, which will represent the bottom line. The second closest will be the second line up, and so on.

When you can see which hexagram you have cast, look it up in the text. The Judgment, Commentary, and Image will answer your question.

However, the six wands methods does not offer 'moving lines', so the Lines cannot be taken into account, and you cannot obtain a further hexagram.

Interpreting the Moving Lines

The occurrence of moving lines not only adds significance to the original hexagram but carries you on to a second hexagram. For example, assume you divided and counted the sticks as instructed and came up with this result:

5 + 4 + 8	▬▬ ▬▬
9 + 8 + 4	▬▬▬▬▬
5 + 4 + 8	▬▬ ▬▬
9 + 4 + 4	▬▬ ▬▬
5 + 8 + 4	▬▬ ▬▬
5 + 4 + 8	▬▬ ▬▬

This gives you Hexagram No 8, Pi, Seeking unity. But suppose you came up with this:

5 + 4 + 8	▬▬ ▬▬
9 + 8 + 4	▬▬▬▬▬
9 + 8 + 8	▬▬x▬▬
9 + 4 + 4	▬▬ ▬▬
5 + 8 + 4	▬▬ ▬▬
9 + 8 + 8	▬▬x▬▬

This will still give you Pi, but it includes two 'moving' lines – the bottom line and the fourth line up. Read the Judgment, Commentary, and Image accompanying Pi, followed by the texts for the first (reading from the bottom up) and the fourth line.

Now, change the two moving lines into their opposites. In both cases here an Old Yin line will become a Young Yang. You now have a second hexagram, No 17, Sui, Allegiance.

It may also be worthwhile discovering what happens if the moving lines are changing at different times. If the Old Yin in the bottom line changes into a Young Yang first, you will obtain hexagram No 3, Chun, Initial difficulties. But if the Old Yin in the fourth line changes first, you will obtain hexagram No 45, Ts'ui, Congregation.

1. 乾 I Ch'ien
Creative Principle

THE TRIGRAMS
ABOVE: Ch'ien Heaven, the creative
BELOW: Ch'ien Heaven, the creative
Ch'ien represents what is great, penetrating, advantageous, correct and firm. It is the originator, the creative. The hexagram consists entirely of yang lines, with the qualities of creativity, virility, activity and strength. There is no weakness or yielding. It is a double image of the trigram heaven (or origination). It embodies the inner creative power of the lower trigram, representing that of man, and the outer creativity of the upper trigram, that of heaven.

THE JUDGMENT
Ch'ien works sublime success. Perserverance brings favourable results to he who is firm and unyielding.

COMMENTARY
Vast is the great originator. All things owe their beginning to it, and it contains all the meanings embodied in its name: the clouds move and the rain falls everywhere; all things appear in their developed form. The initiated comprehend the relationship between beginning and end, and how each of the six lines reaches its accomplishment at the appointed time. At the proper hour, they mount the chariot drawn by these six dragons and drive across the sky.

Ch'ien transforms everything, developing its true nature as heaven determines, preserving great harmony in union. The initiate appears, high above all things, and everything under heaven enjoys true repose.

THE IMAGE
The movement of the heavens reveals transcendent power. The superior man, therefore, makes himself strong and indefatigable.

THE LINES
In the bottom line, NINE signifies:
The dragon lies concealed in the deep. Action at such a time would be unwise.
The superior man is represented by a dragon, symbolising energy in nature. The time of action is near, but the wise man bides his time.

In the second line, NINE signifies:
The dragon appears in the field. It is a favourable time to see the great man.
Although the superior man may begin in a subordinate position, his purpose will raise him to a state of power, where others will benefit from it.

In the third line, NINE signifies:
The superior man is active all day long. At nightfall his mind is still full of care. Danger, but no reproach.
The great man's importance grows, but he must not allow ambition to destroy his integrity. Remaining aware of what lies ahead, he will avoid all pitfalls.

In the fourth line, NINE signifies:
The flight across the abyss is not sure. He who is resolute suffers no reproach.
The great man can launch himself into the world or retire into contemplation. As long as he is true to his nature, he will not be blamed for anything.

In the fifth line, NINE signifies:
The dragon flies across the heavens. It is a favourable time to see the great man.
All nature is in accord. The great man has made his choice, and everyone watches him as he reaches the height of his achievement.

In the sixth line, NINE signifies:
The dragon flies too high. There will be cause for repentance.
Here is a warning not to aspire too high, allowing arrogance to isolate the great man from the rest of mankind.

2. 坤 K'un
The Passive Principle

THE TRIGRAMS
ABOVE: K'un Earth, the passive
BELOW: K'un Earth, the passive
K'un represents also what is great, penetrating, advantageous, correct, and having the firmness of the mare. The hexagram consists entirely of yin lines – feminine, yielding, and shaded. It is the diametrical opposite of Ch'ien in structure but complements it in character: male and female, heaven and earth, spirit and matter, the creative and the passive principle, are nothing but two aspects of the same whole.

THE JUDGMENT
K'un brings supreme success through steadfast acceptance. When the superior man takes the initiative in action he will go astray; if he follows, he will find his true leader. It is advantageous to find friends in the west and south, and to relinquish friends in the north and east. Quiet perseverance brings good fortune to the superior man.

COMMENTARY
The creativity of K'un is complete: all things owe their birth to it, and it obediently accepts the influences of heaven, supporting and containing everything. The mare is an earthly creature: she moves about without restriction, mild and docile, strong and well-favoured. So should the superior man behave.

THE IMAGE
K'un denotes the great capacity and sustaining power of the earth. The superior man, therefore, employs his virtue in supporting all men and all things.

THE LINES
In the bottom line, SIX signifies:
He treads only on hoarfrost, but solid ice is near.
The wise man, finding that his steps take him on to newly frozen water, retraces his path and bides his time until the ice is strong enough.

In the second line, SIX signifies:
Straight, square, great; line, plane, solid. Purposeless, the work still goes forward.
Allowing himself to be carried forward by the progress of nature, the superior man proceeds toward his destiny.

In the third line, SIX signifies:
Although the line is hidden, it persists; who serves a king should do his work and not seek fame.
The wise man isn't leaves fame to others. He does not impose his ideas on others, but perseveres at his tasks, confident that true virtue will be recognised.

In the fourth line, SIX signifies:
A tightly tied sack. No praise, but no reproach.
The sack keeps its secrets. The wise man keeps himself to himself, whether in solitude or in the midst of the world's turmoil.

In the fifth line, SIX signifies:
A yellow undergarment: Supreme good fortune.
Yellow is the colour of the earth and symbolises sincerity. An undergarment is not shown off. One in a high but subordinate position should be discreet.

In the sixth line, SIX signifies:
Dragons fight in the field. Their blood is black and yellow.
When one attempts to fight a way into a position higher than that to which one is entitled, both sides will suffer injury.

Initial Difficulties

THE TRIGRAMS
ABOVE: K'an deep dangerous water
BELOW: Chen thunder and awakening
The sign for Chun represents a new shoot, struggling to burst its way through the soil in the first days of spring. The lower trigram, Chen, represents upward movement, and its image is thunder. The upper trigram, K'an, has a downward movement and its image is rain. There is chaotic confusion: the air is filled with thunder and rain; but the thunderstorm brings release from tension, and everything is calm again.

THE JUDGMENT
Initial difficulties are followed by supreme success, the result of acting firmly and correctly. Nothing should be attempted without appointing those who can provide appropriate assistance.

COMMENTARY
In Chun we see the intercourse begin of Ch'ien the strong and K'un the weak, and the difficulties that arise. Motion in the midst of danger leads on to success. By the action of the thunder and rain, all the space between heaven and earth is filled up. But the time is still full of disorder and obscure: nothing can be predicted with confidence. It is advantageous to appoint deputies and helpers, but it is unwise to suppose that the storm is at an end and that rest and peace are at hand.

THE IMAGE
Clouds and thunder represent the idea of initial difficulty. The superior man busies himself with creating order out of confusion.

THE LINES
In the bottom line, NINE signifies:
Obstacles and hesitation before action. Perseverance is rewarding.
When obstacles are met at the beginning of an enterprise, the best course may well be inaction and calculation.

In the second line, SIX signifies:
Difficulties increase. One of the horses breaks free from her wagon. But he is not a highwayman, he is one who wishes her to be his wife. The chaste maiden rejects his advances, and waits ten years before she bears children.
The man who offers help must be rejected, because it will conflict with free decision making. Later the right moment will present itself.

In the third line, SIX signifies:
He hunts deer in the forest without a guide and loses his way. The superior man, understanding the situation, gives up the chase. To continue brings humiliation.
Obstinately pursuing a goal without seeking advice is bound to result in failure.

In the fourth line, SIX signifies:
The horses break from the wagon. She seeks the assistance of her suitor. The time is auspicious for going forward.
There is a wrong time and a right time to accept help. It may mean that pride must be swallowed, but there is no shame in accepting help.

In the fifth line, NINE signifies:
Obstacles to generosity. A little perseverance brings success. Much perseverance brings misfortune.
The individual's gestures are misinterpreted, but he must not try to force the outcome: through confident actions he will overcome the obstacles.

In the sixth line, SIX signifies:
The horses drag the wagon back. Tears of blood are wept.
The difficulties have been too great: the only way is back to the beginning. But success is not achieved by giving up; another way will be found.

4. 蒙 Meng
Youthful Inexperience

THE TRIGRAMS
ABOVE: Ken mountain, stillness
BELOW: K'an dangerous deep water
As Chun represents the infant plant struggling
to break the surface, so Meng represents its
undeveloped appearance. The water bubbling
up at the foot of the mountain is the image of
inexperienced youth. When the spring firsts
bursts out, it has no idea where it is going; but its
determined flow eventually fills up the deep, and
it goes on its way.

THE JUDGMENT
There will be progress and success. I do not seek
out the young and inexperienced; he comes to find
me. When he first asks my advice, I instruct him.
But if he comes a second or a third time, that is
troublesome, and I do not advise the troublesome.
Firm and correct action brings favourable results.

COMMENTARY
Uncultivated growth. The dangerous pit lies at
the foot of the mountain, and to stay on the edge
of the abyss is youthful folly. There are perils and
obstacles in the way of progress, but the young and
inexperienced should be nurtured like a new plant.
The intention of the novice is accomplished.

THE IMAGE
As the spring gushes out at the foot of the
mountain, so the superior man improves his
character by diligent thoroughness in all
his actions.

THE LINES
In the bottom line, SIX signifies:
*The ignorant youth should be disciplined, but remove
his fetters lest he be humiliated.* Severe treatment is
of great help in dispelling folly. But too much
discipline will degenerate into tyranny.

In the second line, NINE signifies:
To suffer fools kindly brings good fortune.
Understanding of women brings good fortune.
The son can take charge of the household.
The young man who begins to understand the
importance of the tolerance shown by his elders,
will soon be able to take on their responsibilities.

In the third line, SIX signifies:
No good will come of a maiden who loses control
When she sees a man of bronze. Do not cherish her.
Like a girl throwing herself at a heroic figure,
the inexperienced man may lose all individuality
by trying to imitate a stronger personality.

In the fourth line, SIX signifies:
Bound in the chains of his ignorance,
He suffers humiliation and regret.
The youth can easily entangle himself in fantasies
which will only result in confusion. Rejecting help,
he must be left to return to reality by himself.

In the fifth line, SIX signifies:
The simplicity of the child brings good fortune.
Inexperience is best overcome by seeking
he teacher in a spirit of humility.

In the sixth line, NINE signifies:
Punishing the inexperienced youth,
One should not injure him.
Punishment should not be imposed in anger.
It is for the good of the ignorant, not to
relieve the conscience of the teacher.

<h1>5. 需 Hsü</h1>
<h1>Patient Anticipation</h1>

THE TRIGRAMS
ABOVE: K'an dangerous deep water
BELOW: Ch'ien Heaven, the creative
Water is seen in the heavens in the form of
clouds. But clouds, though they promise rain, also
indicate that we must wait for that promise to be
fulfilled. The trigrams, symbolising danger above
but strength within, also draw attention to the
importance of biding one's time.

THE JUDGMENT
Waiting. With sincerity, there will follow brilliant
success. Perseverance brings good fortune. It is
advantageous to cross the great water.

COMMENTARY
The dangerous deep of K'an lies ahead, and
though the creative power of Ch'ien drives him
forward, he must show patience. Only then will the
time come when he can go forward and achieve his
goal with success. A journey – not necessarily across
water, it may be a spiritual one – will be rewarding.

THE IMAGE
Clouds rise up to heaven, representing patient
anticipation. The superior man, accordingly,
spends the time in eating and drinking, satisfying
himself and remaining cheerful.

THE LINES
In the bottom line, NINE signifies:
*He waits at the edge of the meadow. And furthers his
plans by remaining still. No reproach.*
Danger is still far off: the prudent man does not
advance into the open but prepares himself for
future action.

In the second line, NINE signifies:
*He waits on the sandy bank of the mountain
stream. There are rumours of scandal,
But in the end, good fortune.*
A steadfast calmness in the face of false and
malicious statements will bring success at last.

In the third line, NINE signifies:
He waits in the mud, expecting the arrival of the enemy.
The ground is slippery and treacherous, but now
the peril must be faced with as much preparation
as possible.

In the fourth line, SIX signifies:
*He waits standing in blood,
But he will escape from the pit.*
Disaster threatens and waiting with brave
composure for fate to take its course is the only
way out.

In the fifth line, NINE signifies:
He waits at the table. Perseverance brings good fortune.
The still eye of the storm. The wise man
uses the time to recover his strength
to meet the struggles to come.

In the sixth line, SIX signifies:
*He falls into the pit. Three unexpected guests arrive:
Receive them with respect and all will be well in the end.*
All seems lost. but help comes from an
unexpected source. It may not be recognised for
what it is, but the wise man will welcome it.

6. 訟 Sung
Conflict

THE TRIGRAMS
ABOVE: Ch'ien Heaven, the creative
BELOW: K'an dangerous deep water
The upper trigram represents heaven, which tends to move upward; while the lower trigram, representing water, always moves downward. So the two halves of Chun pull away from one another, producing a situation of tension and incipient conflict. The attribute of the male Ch'ien is strength, that of K'an is subtlety and intrigue; a character combining outward determination with inward cunning will be a quarrelsome one.

THE JUDGMENT
Conflict. Confidence is obstructed, and a cautious halt at the halfway stage will bring good fortune. But obstinate determination to go forward against all obstacles can only end in misfortune. It is a favourable time to see the great man, but it is unsafe to cross the great water.

COMMENTARY
No matter what the sincerity of a man's motives, it is impossible to avoid the conflict, but the danger can be mitigated by a cautious approach. The prudent man remains clear-headed and inwardly strong, recognising that his only course lies in meeting his opponent halfway, and that the conflict must not be allowed to become permanent. Advice from the great man strengthens his position, but if he attempts to go forward across the water he will fall into the abyss.

THE IMAGE
Heaven and water moving in opposite ways are the image of conflict. The superior man therefore appraises the beginning of any venture with great care.

THE LINES
In the bottom line, SIX signifies:
If the conflict is not prosecuted, there will be some gossip; But, in the end, good fortune.
Facing opposition, the prudent man keeps his opinion to himself. This might cause some gossip, but ultimately the enterprise will reach fruition.

In the second line, NINE signifies:
He cannot continue the conflict, but yields and returns home. His fellow townsmen. Three hundred households. Suffer no reproach.
To retreat in the face of superior strength is no disgrace.

In the third line, SIX signifies:
He nourishes himself on the ancient virtues, and remains firm and constant. There is danger, but good fortune at last. Who serves a king should do his work and not seek fame.
He who adheres to the established code of conduct may find himself in danger of losing his position, but success will come in the end.

In the fourth line, NINE signifies:
He cannot continue the conflict, but gives way and submits to fate; changing his disposition, he finds peace in perseverance. Good fortune.
Unsatisfied with his situation, the man attempts to improve it by struggle. But only by accepting his destiny does he find peace and success.

In the fifth line, NINE signifies:
To engage in conflict before a just judge brings supreme success.
When the cause for conflict is good, the judgment of an impartial man will bring great good fortune.

In the sixth line, NINE signifies:
Though he gains the leather belt, three times before noon it will be taken from him.
Although he has won the leather belt – the victor's trophy – others attack him repeatedly and the result is unending conflict.

7. 師 Shih
A Troop of Soldiers

THE TRIGRAMS
ABOVE: **K'un** Earth, the passive
BELOW: **K'an** dangerous deep water
Water lies beneath the earth, like a subterranean stream about to rise to the surface as a spring. So the soldiers lie hidden when they are not needed, but ready to burst into action. The trigrams, combining inner danger with outer devotion, are also symbolic of military organisation.

THE JUDGMENT
With firm and correct action, and a leader of age and experience, there will be resultant good fortune without reproach.

COMMENTARY
The name of Shih describes the multitude of the host. The firmness and correctness indicated by the hexagram refer to moral strength. The man who can lead the army is fit to be king, because the strong line in the lower trigram holds the whole together and everything responds to his control. Proceeding with a dangerous task is a means to winning the allegiance of the people and the control of the kingdom. The results may distress the whole countryside, but in the face of good fortune how can any error arise?

THE IMAGE
Water hidden in the earth is the image of the army. The superior man, accordingly, wins followers by his generosity.

THE LINES
In the bottom line, SIX signifies:
The soldiers must set out in good order; if there is disorder, there will be misfortune.
Discipline and strategy is the essential of all military organisations, and the secret of victory.

In the second line, NINE signifies:
He stands surrounded by his forces. There is good fortune, and no reproach. Three times the king awards battle honours.
The leader should always be in the midst of his army. Success is only ensured if he plans to share the profits with his associates.

In the third line, SIX signifies:
The army that carries corpses in its wagons is assured of failure.
An army must be able to move quickly and easily. The army that carries its dead with it is already defeated.

In the fourth line, SIX signifies:
The army retreats but there is no disgrace.
There is no shame is withdrawing in the face of superior force.

In the fifth line, SIX signifies:
When wild beasts roam the field, there is no disgrace in capturing them. The eldest son is in command, the youngest carries away the dead: persistence brings misfortune.
While the victorious enemy is occupied looting the battlefield, attack them, but be ready to retreat before the enemy counterattacks.

In the sixth line, SIX signifies:
The king issues his commands, grants estates and titles of nobility; but power should not be given to the inferior.
After victory, the rank and file should not be given land and authority, because their inexperience may mean that they rule badly.

Seeking Unity

THE TRIGRAMS
ABOVE: K'an dangerous deep water
BELOW: K'un Earth, the passive
The reverse of the previous hexagram, Shih, where the water lay beneath the earth. Now the water lies on the earth, flowing towards other water, forming streams that unite into rivers and rivers that flow into the seas. All the lines of this hexagram, except the fifth (the place of the ruler), are feminine and yielding. It is the fifth line that holds them together as they flow.

THE JUDGMENT
Unity brings good fortune. Consult the oracle again to discover whether you possess true grace, constancy and perseverance; then there is no reproach. Those who are irresolute will gradually come to him; but delaying too long will lead to misfortune.

COMMENTARY
The hexagram represents inferiors docilely following the lead of the superior man. Indeed, his equals and his superiors will also follow him, because a strong man is needed to hold the people together. Those who first join him will take part in forming organisations and the laws that bind them; latecomers will be unable to share in the good fortune of the community.

THE IMAGE
Water upon the earth is the image of holding together. Ancient kings granted land to their principal followers, and maintained friendly relations with their princes.

THE LINES
In the bottom line, SIX signifies:
True loyalty is without reproach. When the breast is as full of sincerity as a flowing bowl, good fortune comes from far away.
The inner strength of the sincere man will attract unexpected good fortune from without.

In the second line, SIX signifies:
The movement to unity comes from within. Righteous persistence brings good fortune.
When a man understands his true nature, he will join with others not as a servant but as an equal.

In the third line, SIX signifies:
He joins with those who are unfit.
We must beware of entering into associations with people who surround us, but who are not of our way of thinking.

In the fourth line, SIX signifies:
Join with the leader. Righteous persistence brings good fortune.
The wise man will join a leader, but he must remain constant and not allow himself to be led astray.

In the fifth line, NINE signifies:
This is the sign of union. The king hunts with beaters on three sides only, losing the game that runs before him. The people need no threats and there is good fortune.
In royal hunts the game was driven only from three sides, so that some had an opportunity to escape. A well-governed citizenry needs no coercion.

In the sixth line, SIX signifies:
There is no leader, no union. Great misfortune.
No enterprise can succeed without strong leadership.

9. 小畜 Hsiao Ch'u
The Power of the Weak

THE TRIGRAMS
ABOVE: Sun wind, gentleness, penetration
BELOW: Ch'ien Heaven, the creative
The hexagram represents the ability, even of the weak, to restrain and impede. The five strong yang lines are held in check by the yin line in the fourth place, the position of the minister.

THE JUDGMENT
Success lies in the power of the weak. Dense clouds gather, but there is no rain from the western borders.

COMMENTARY
Hsiao Ch'u combines the symbols of strength and flexibility. The weak line in the fourth position occupies its proper place, and the strong lines above and below it show that there will be progress and success, at the same time conferring freedom upon their subjects. 'Dense clouds but no rain' indicates a strong forward movement, but a movement that has not yet reached its culmination.

THE IMAGE
The wind drives across the sky, crowding the clouds together. The superior man, accordingly, reveals his virtuous qualities to all.

THE LINES
In the bottom line, NINE signifies:
How could there be reproach in returning to the true way? Success lies in this.
The 'true way' is the Tao, the path of correctness. The superior man follows the path on which he can advance or retreat as he wishes.

In the second line, NINE signifies:
Persuaded to retrace his steps, he finds success.
He who can accept that the best course is to retreat in the face of inauspicious events will bring good fortune in the end.

In the third line, NINE signifies:
The spokes of the wagon wheel are broken, husband and wife stand glowering at each other.
The man has suffered a serious accident and has ignored the advice of the weaker party. But in quarrelling, he sacrifices his dignity.

In the fourth line, SIX signifies:
If he shows confidence, fear and bloodshed are avoided. There is no reproach.
Confident that he is pursuing the correct course, the wise man steers a way that avoids catastrophe.

In the fifth line, NINE signifies:
Sincerity and loyalty make for good neighbours.
In the weaker person, loyalty means devotion; in the stronger, sincerity breeds trust. Complementing each other, the bond is stronger.

In the sixth line, NINE signifies:
The rains come, and there is rest at last, for he has followed his way. But persistence puts the women in danger, for the moon is nearly full. And if the superior man goes forth, there is misfortune.
The wind, continually driving the clouds together, finally brings the rain. One must be content with what has already been attained.

10. 履 Lü
Treading Wisely

THE TRIGRAMS
ABOVE: Ch'ien Heaven, the creative
BELOW: Tui A pool of water, joy
Lu means both the proper conduct and, literally, treading upon something. Here the strong, the father principle of Ch'ien, stands upon Tui, which represents the youngest daughter; but, at the same time, the lower trigram Tui stands upon its own firm base and (as it were) treads upwards against the weight above. This is a symbol of the love and joy that exist between a father and his favourite daughter.

THE JUDGMENT
He treads upon the tail of the tiger, but it does not bite him. Success.

COMMENTARY
Weakness treads upon strength. But pleasure and satisfaction respond to strength, so there is no danger. He is raised to a high position, responding to heaven's will, and cannot be harmed or distressed. He shines in glory.

THE IMAGE
Heaven above, the pool below: the image of treading. The superior man, consulting both high and low, knows his proper place and gains the approbation of the people.

THE LINES
In the bottom line, NINE signifies:
He goes forward in simplicity. There is no reproach.
Common conventions have little meaning for the man who takes simplicity and truth as his guidelines.

In the second line, NINE signifies:
The man in darkness treads a smooth and level path, And finds good fortune.
The 'man in darkness' asks nothing of anyone. Self-sufficient, he is content and fortune smiles upon him.

In the third line, SIX signifies:
Even a one-eyed man can see, a lame man can walk; He treads on the tail of the tiger and is bitten. Misfortune. The champion plays the part of the king.
No-one should attempt to push ahead beyond the limit of his abilities.

In the fourth line, NINE signifies:
He treads on the tail of the tiger, but caution and circumspection bring good fortune in the end.
Only the man who knows what he is doing dare tread upon the tiger's tail without punishment.

In the fifth line, NINE signifies:
He treads with care. Persistence. But consciousness of danger.
One must be firm in conduct, but there is still danger and obstinate perseverance is perilous unless the danger is well understood.

In the sixth line, NINE signifies:
Watching his step and the length of the path that he treads, heeding the favourable omens, brings great good fortune.
The enterprise nears completion. The wise man examines the way he has come, and what lies before him, understanding what to expect.

11. 泰 T'ai

Peace

THE TRIGRAMS
ABOVE: K'un Earth, the passive
BELOW: Ch'ien Heaven, the creative
The feminine creative, which moves downwards, is above; the male creative, which moves upwards, is below. Thus they combine their influences and produce harmony. This hexagram represents the first month of spring.

THE JUDGMENT
The small declines, and the great and good is coming. Good fortune and success.

COMMENTARY
Celestial and terrestrial forces are in communion with one another, and all things move without restraint. High and low, superiors and inferiors, sharing the same aims, are in harmony with one another. Yang, representing strength, lies within; yin, representing joyous acceptance, lies without. The superior man is at the centre of things, his fortune increasing, while those of mean nature are at the edges, declining in their influence.

THE IMAGE
Heaven and earth unite, forming T'ai, the symbol of peace. In such a way a mighty ruler regulates the separate ways of heaven and earth, marking the seasons and the divisions of space. By this he brings assistance to people on every side.

THE LINES
In the bottom line, NINE signifies:
When the grass is pulled up, roots and the sod come with it. Each in his own way finds success in his enterprise.
In favourable times, the man who is called to public service brings like-minded people with him, whose common aim will be the welfare of the people.

In the second line, NINE signifies:
He deals gently with the uncultured, crosses the river without a boat, is undismayed by the distance, and does not favour his companions. This is the way to tread the middle path.
The superior man can find a use for everything, and is not dismayed by the shortcomings of others because the great can make use of the imperfect.

In the third line, NINE signifies:
There is no plain not followed by a hill, no departure not followed by a return. He who persists in the face of danger is without reproach. Do not despair at the inevitability of change; a setback may be a blessing.
As long as a man remains superior to what fate may bring him, fortune will not desert him.

In the fourth line, SIX signifies:
He flutters down, not boasting of his riches. Joins with his neighbours, frank and sincere.
In times of peace and prosperity, those in high places mix with the more lowly as equals out of genuine spontaneity.

In the fifth line, SIX signifies:
I am the emperor I giving his daughter in marriage. This brings blessings and great good fortune.
In bestowing his most precious possession upon one of his subjects, the emperor brings fortune by its wise and modest combination of high and low.

In the sixth line, SIX signifies:
The city wall tumbles into the moat. Now is not time for an army. Give orders to your own people. Though this is the correct course, reproach cannot be avoided.
Peace is at an end but passive resistance is the best option. Nevertheless, there will be cause for regret.

12. 否 P'i
Stagnation

THE TRIGRAMS
ABOVE: Ch'ien Heaven, the creative
BELOW: K'un Earth, the passive
The opposite of the preceding T'ai: heaven is above, moving further and further away, and earth sinks below. P'i is associated with the seventh month, when the year is already in decline.

THE JUDGMENT
Stagnation. Evil doers work against the perseverance of the superior man. The great and good withdraws, and the inferior advances.

COMMENTARY
Heaven and earth are not in proper communion with one another; and so there is lack of understanding between all kinds of men, matters do not have free course, and conditions are unfavourable to the firm and correct behaviour of the superior man. The inner trigram is made up of weak yin lines, and the outer of strong yang lines. So the way of the inferior appears to be increasing, and that of the superior waning.

THE IMAGE
Heaven and earth stand divided, the image of stagnation. The wise man withdraws into himself and conceals his true quality. In this way he avoids the calamities that threaten him; but he will not be rewarded or honoured.

THE LINES
In the bottom line, SIX signifies:
When the grass is pulled up, roots and the sod come with it. Each in his own way finds success by perseverance.
Almost exactly the same text as the first line of T'ai, here the implication is of a man persuading others to join him in retirement.

In the second line, SIX signifies:
They suffer and obey; thus inferior people find good fortune. But the superior man uses the time of stagnation To achieve success.
Those in lower positions would gladly be instructed by the wise man. But unable to improve matters, he keeps himself to himself, preserving his strength.

In the third line, SIX signifies:
He conceals the shame in his breast.
One of inferior standing has seized power, but he has no dominion over others and is ashamed. But self-realization is the first step to recovery.

In the fourth line, NINE signifies:
He who answers a call from on high is without reproach. Those who follow him will benefit.
The man who leads the people out of the depths must feel the call.

In the fifth line, NINE signifies:
Stagnation is coming to an end. There is great fortune for the great man. What if we fail? What if we fail? Then bind it to a clump of mulberry shoots.
When a mulberry bush is cut back, strong shoots sprout from the base: tying something to the shoots symbolises making success certain.

In the sixth line, NINE signifies:
Stagnation is ended. Stagnation began it, but now there is good fortune.
Constant effort is needed to maintain peace, and if left to itself it will decline into decadence and stagnation again.

13. 同人 T'ung Jen
Companions

THE TRIGRAMS
ABOVE: Ch'ien Heaven the creative
BELOW: Li fire, brightness
It is the nature of the fire to burn upwards into heaven, symbolising the concept of fellowship or love. The yin line in the second place gives the hexagram its central character, its yielding quality serving to hold together the five yang lines that surround it. This hexagram is the complement of hexagram number 7 (Shih the Troop of Soldiers). Shih has danger within and obedience surrounding it, the image of the unquestioning army; but T'ung Jen is clarity within and strength without, the image of a brotherhood held together by its own firmness.

THE JUDGMENT
Fellowship and openness mean success. It is advantageous to cross the great water. Persevering in all things, the superior man advances.

COMMENTARY
T'ung Jen appears in the distant parts of the country, indicating progress and success, 'crossing the great water' symbolising any important journey. Someone weak comes to a position of power, taking centrestage and responding to the creative power. Such a person may be known as the beloved. The central yang line in the upper trigram represents the superior man, the only one who can understand and affect the thinking of all the people.

THE IMAGE
Heaven and fire together symbolise companionship. The superior man, accordingly, organises the people and distinguishes things according to their kinds and classes.

Heaven moves upwards, just as fire does, but it is very different from fire. As the stars in the sky mark the divisions of time, so human society and all things that belong together must be ordered. Companionship is not just a gathering together of like-minded people: there must be organisation of the diversity.

THE LINES
In the bottom line, NINE signifies:
Companionship begins with those at the gate.
No reproach.
The beginning of union among different people should occur where everyone can see and be seen and are on an equal footing.

In the second line, SIX signifies:
The family bands together. Humiliation.
Forming factions is the first sign of a struggle for power. Out of this will come failure and disgrace.

In the third line, NINE signifies:
He hides his weapons in the thicket, watching from the top of a high hill.
When factions are formed, no man trusts another. For a long time he waits, hoping to catch his opponents by surprise, but there is no joy in this.

In the fourth line, NINE signifies:
He climbs upon his battlements because he cannot fight. But good fortune is near.
The wise man does not make the mistake of attacking his opponents, and soon all will be well.

In the fifth line, NINE signifies:
Lovers begin by weeping and lamenting but in the end they laugh. The struggles of many bring them together.
Any association will begin with troubles, but once resolved the companions will find happiness.

In the sixth line, NINE signifies:
The beloved is in a distant place. No regrets.
The companions trust one another, even when far apart. But the fact that the beloved is in a distant place means that the association is not yet fulfilled.

14. 大有 Ta Yu
Abundant Possessions

THE TRIGRAMS
ABOVE: Li Fire, brightness
BELOW: Ch'ien Heaven, the creative
Here the flame burns in the highest heaven, revealing all things in its light. The weak yin line is in the place of the ruler, indicating that wealth comes to the man who is modest and benevolent, even though he occupies a high position.

THE JUDGMENT
Ta Yu indicates wealth in abundance, and also great success.

COMMENTARY
As in the preceding hexagram, T'ung Jen, it is the weak yin line that holds the hexagram together, and occupies the most important position. The virtues of the hexagram are strength and vigour combined with elegance and brightness. Because it responds to heaven, performing all things at the proper time, it indicates great progress and success.

THE IMAGE
Fire in the heavens above is the image of possession in abundance. The superior man, obeying the benevolent will of heaven, suppresses evil and advances the virtuous.

THE LINES
In the bottom line, NINE signifies:
He has no communion with evil. Remaining blameless; Keeping conscious of difficulty, he averts reproach.
Wealth can be utterly destructive if a wealthy man is led astray.

In the second line, NINE signifies:
Big wagons are for loading. He may attempt any enterprise without reproach.
There is no fear of failure for lack of resources, but one who undertakes a great venture must be ready for any eventuality.

In the third line, NINE signifies:
A prince offers all to the emperor. But this is not in a small man's power.
A truly magnanimous man should devote his possessions to the good of the people.

In the fourth line, NINE signifies:
He distinguishes himself from his neighbours. No blame.
A rich, powerful man among other rich, powerful men must remain aloof, but not out of a false sense of pride.

In the fifth line, SIX signifies:
He who is sincere and accessible, but maintains his dignity, will gain great honours.
The hearts of the people are won, not by force and repression, but by benevolence and philanthropy.

In the sixth line, NINE signifies:
Giving and receiving. Blessed by the heavens. He enjoys great good fortune.
The great man gives from his wealth and receives the thanks of others; they give their love and receive his protection.

Humility

THE TRIGRAMS
ABOVE: **K'un** Earth, the receptive
BELOW: **Ken** mountain, stillness
Ken, the mountain, dispenses the gifts of heaven, the rain that falls from the clouds around its peak, and shines in the clear air. Ken represents the modesty of great men. K'un, the earth, is exalted, symbolising the way simple men are raised up by modesty.

THE JUDGMENT
Humility engenders success. The superior man, understanding this, enjoys a satisfactory outcome to his undertakings.

COMMENTARY
Ch'ien symbolises progress and success, because it is heaven's way to send down its good influences and shed radiance, and it is earth's way to send its influences upwards. So it is also heaven's way to reduce the over-full and augment the modest; as it is earth's way to throw down the full and raise up the humble. The demons and gods abominate the over-full and bless the modest, as it is the way of men to hate the full and love the humble. Modesty in a high position shines still more brilliantly; there is nothing higher. As the mountain is hidden by the earth, so the wise man hides his abilities and wealth with proper humility.

THE IMAGE
Within the earth, there is a mountain, the image of humility. The superior man reduces that which is too much, and increases that which is too little, setting one in the scale to balance the other.

THE LINES
In the bottom line, SIX signifies:
The superior man is even modest about his modesty. He may cross the great water and find good fortune.
Those who approach a problem without pride or concern for their standing will solve it quickly and simply.

In the second line, SIX signifies:
Modesty itself achieves recognition. Persistence brings good fortune.

In the third line, NINE signifies:
The superior man is recognised but maintains his humility. He brings all matters to conclusion. Good fortune.
The wise man is not dazzled by fame but remains humble.

In the fourth line, SIX signifies:
Proper humility and nothing that is not proper humility in all his actions.
True modesty is the sign of confidence in one's position; it should not be permitted to degenerate into servility.

In the fifth line, SIX signifies:
Employ your neighbours without boasting of your riches. Attack with vigour. All is propitious.
However modest a man, he who occupies a position of responsibility must engage the help of others to carry out his plans.

In the sixth line, SIX signifies:
Modesty achieves recognition. He sets his army on the march but only to punish his own city and land.
It is difficult for a modest man to impose his will upon others. But, provided the discipline is just, he will be honoured for his actions.

16. 豫 Yü
Anticipation

THE TRIGRAMS
ABOVE: Chen thunder and awakening
BELOW: K'un Earth, the receptive
Chen's characteristics are movement and danger; the
K'un's characteristics are passivity and obedience.
The movement, meeting devotion, inspires enthusiasm.
The strong yang line in the fourth place (that of the
minister), demands obedience from all the weak
yin lines; but there is an inherent danger in this
arrangement.

THE JUDGMENT
It is advantageous to establish a number of tributary
princes, and place the army in a state of readiness.

COMMENTARY
The thunder awakes in heaven, and the earth is docile
below. The sun and the moon keep their courses,
and the four seasons do not change their appointed
times. So action according to the will of heaven gives
rise to anticipation and calm confidence. The sage
also follows heaven's will, and the people follow his
judgment with little need for punishment or for any
form of penalty. Great indeed are the moment and the
meaning of Yü!

THE IMAGE
Thunder bursts from the earth into heaven. In such
a way did the ancient kings honour heaven and its
supreme lord with solemn music and appropriate
sacrifice, remembering their revered ancestors.

THE LINES
In the bottom line, SIX signifies:
He proclaims his anticipation of pleasure. An evil omen.
The lowly person looks forward selfishly to his own
satisfaction and so invites misfortune.

In the second line, SIX signifies:
*He is firm as a rock but not the whole day. Persistence
brings success.*
The wise man is not led away by illusion and knows
the right moment to move.

In the third line, SIX signifies:
*Ignorant anticipation brings regrets. Hesitation leads
to repentance.*
The inferior man places his reliance upon those
above him without understanding that he too should
take action.

In the fourth line, NINE signifies:
*He is the source of harmony and satisfaction, and achieves
great things. Have no doubts. Gather friends around you
as the clasp gathers the hair.*
The superior man is an inspiration to all through his
confidence and freedom from hesitation.

In the fifth line, SIX signifies:
He is constantly sick but does not die.
Continuing to look forward, he finds himself
obstructed. But provided he does not expend his
anticipation in empty enthusiasm he will survive.

In the sixth line, SIX signifies:
*His anticipation is deluded, devoted to self-satisfaction;
but if he changes his course, even when all seems completed,
there is no blame.*
It is easy to be led astray by foolish enthusiasm,
but even at the last moment an awakening can save
the situation.

17. 隨 Sui
Allegiance

THE TRIGRAMS

ABOVE: Tui a pool of water, joy
BELOW: Chen thunder and awakening

Above is joy, the youngest daughter; below is awakening, the eldest son. So the awakening interest of the older man is excited by the joyous movement of the young girl; he defers to her and shows her consideration, but in due course she will follow him.

THE JUDGMENT

Compliance in the beginning leads to ultimate success. Firmness and rectitude are advantageous, and there is no blame.

COMMENTARY

In Sui, the strong trigram places itself below the weak; in the two we see the combination of movement and pleasure. The whole universe complies with what the hour dictates: a leader must adjust his actions to the situation; a follower must adjust his actions to those of his leader. But just as the leader should not ask others to follow him unless his path is the right one, so his followers must assure themselves of his rectitude.

THE IMAGE

Thunder rumbles below the surface of the pool. As darkness falls, the superior man goes into his house to rest.

THE LINES

In the bottom line, NINE signifies:
He changes the object of his pursuit. Persistence brings good fortune. Going forth from his door and meeting with those outside, he attains achievement.
The wise man will not follow a belief that is no longer supportable. Listening to others, he must decide whether to be led by others or himself lead.

In the second line, SIX signifies:
He who clings to the little boy loses the strong man.
It is a time to make more mature decisions, and transfer allegiance to a new leader or moral system.

In the third line, SIX signifies:
He who clings to the strong man loses the little boy, but gains what he desires. Persistence is advantageous.
With maturity, one gives up the unmixed happiness of youth, but the wise man is satisfied as he begins to understand what he wants.

In the fourth line, NINE signifies:
Allegiance brings success, but persisting in the same course brings misfortune. Taking his own way with sincerity how can he be blamed?
There are dangers in blind allegiance, both for the followers and for the followed. The leader's only hope is to pursue his course with conviction.

In the fifth line, NINE signifies:
Trusting in goodness. Good fortune.
He who knows what is right must follow it without deviation.

In the sixth line, SIX signifies:
Sincere, he secures allegiance and is himself more firmly bound. The emperor makes sacrifices upon the Western Mountain.
Although he has reached the furthest stages of his development, the sage is constrained by the demands of his followers.

18. 蠱 Ku
Arresting Decay

THE TRIGRAMS
ABOVE: Ken mountain, stillness
BELOW: Sun wind, gentleness
Ku is said to represent 'a bowl in whose contents worms are breeding'. This is because the gentleness of the lower trigram Sun has been covered by the solidity of the upper trigram Ken. In these conditions the expected result is stagnation. But just as decay can be controlled to provide fermentation, so the decay represented by Ku can be arrested and exploited.

THE JUDGMENT
Proper control of decay affords progress and success. It is advantageous to cross the great water. Three days before the beginning; three days after.
[It is important to arrest fermentation before unwelcome decomposition begins. The growth of a new idea may be likened to fermentation.]

COMMENTARY
In Ku we have the strong and immovable above, the weak and pliant below. But control of the processes of decay leads to good order everywhere under heaven, so.that he who goes firmly forward will come to business that must be dealt with. The ending of confusion marks the beginning of order.

THE IMAGE
The wind blows at the foot of the mountain. The superior man, addressing himself to the people, rouses them up and strengthens his resolve.

THE LINES
In the bottom line, six signifies:
A son repairs the errors of his father. A good son, redeeming the reputation of his father. At first, danger, but in the end, good fortune.
The father represents convention, the son youthful vigour, but before the son emerges, there is great danger that the existing system will destroy itself.

In the second line, NINE signifies:
A son repairs the errors of his mother. But he should not be too inflexible.
The errors have not been committed by a strong man, but out of weakness. In setting things right, a degree of kindness and consideration is necessary.

In the third line, nine signifies:
A son repairs the errors of his father. There will be some remorse but no great blame.
The young man has been too hasty in arresting the processes of decay, but too much energy is better than too little.

In the fourth line, six signifies:
The son condones the errors of his father. Persisting, he falls into disgrace.
The indulgent son who lacks the confidence to put right the mistakes of the past will bring humiliation upon himself as well as on his father.

In the fifth line, six signifies:
The son repairs the errors of his father and wins praise.
The true leader receives acclaim for his actions in arresting decay, accepting responsibility for the previous shortcomings of others.

In the sixth line, nine signifies:
He does not serve the emperor but seeks higher goals.
A superior man may not concern himself with worldly affairs but turn his mind to spiritual matters.

19. 臨 Lin
Approaching

THE TRIGRAMS
ABOVE: K'un Earth, the passive
BELOW: Tui a pool of water, joy
Lin is associated with the 12th month of the year, from January to February, when the days begin to lengthen again, and the word *lin* has a number of different meanings that are roughly encompassed by the word 'approaching'. It may be translated as 'becoming great', including the idea of something superior approaching something of lower standing, and from this the idea of a man in high position condescending toward those below him.

THE JUDGMENT
Lin indicates great progress and success; persistence will be advantageous. But in the eighth month there will be misfortune.

COMMENTARY
In Lin we see the strong yang lines moving upwards into the compliance of the upper yin lines. It is a time of joy and hopeful progress as spring approaches; determination and perseverance help us to attain success. But spring and summer are succeeded by autumn, the time of decay, and the next hexagram shows the reversal of this one.

THE IMAGE
The earth above the lake is the image of approaching. The superior man, accordingly, is inexhaustible in his desire to teach, and his tolerance and care for the people are unlimited.

THE LINES
In the bottom line, NINE signifies:
They approach together. Persistence means good fortune.
Good influences begin to exert themselves and like-minded men of goodwill cooperate, but only adherence to what is right will bring ultimate success.

In the second line, NINE signifies:
They approach together. Good fortune: everything is favourable.
The situation is still full of promise: everybody is cooperating, but this is on a material level and there is no true spiritual basis to people's actions.

In the third line, SIX signifies:
He approaches in comfort but gains no advantage. If there is remorse, there is no reproach.
When a man achieves power and influence he may become over confident, but if he recognises his errors in time, he will be free from blame.

In the fourth line, SIX signifies:
They come together. There is no reproach.
A rich and successful man draws a man of acknowledged ability into his own circle.

In the fifth line, SIX signifies:
Wisdom approaches. This is the way of the great prince. Good fortune.
The great ruler must have about him men of ability. In allowing them to exercise their powers, he attains success.

In the sixth line, SIX signifies:
Magnanimity approaches. Good fortune. No reproach.
The great novice returns This means good fortune for all the men he gathers around him; and for himself.

20. 觀 Kuan
Contemplation

THE TRIGRAMS
ABOVE: Sun Wind, gentleness, penetration
BELOW: K'un Earth, the passive
Kuan possesses two related but opposed meanings;
by a slight change in tonal stress it can mean both
contemplating and being contemplated. The dual
implication can be understood thus: someone
who raises himself to a position in which he can
contemplate the rest of humanity at the same time puts
himself up for inspection by the crowd.

THE JUDGMENT
Kuan represents the worshipper who has washed his
hands, but not yet made the offering. Impressed by his
sincerity, everyone looks up to him.

COMMENTARY
Kuan combines the trigrams representing docility and
flexibility; the hexagram is ruled from on high by the
yang lines in fifth and sixth place, and the weak yin
lines look up from below. When we contemplate the
transcendental ways of heaven, we observe how the
four seasons follow one another without deviation.
The sages, pursuing the same way, have given their
instructions, and all under heaven submit to them.

THE IMAGE
The wind moves over the earth. So the kings of old
visited all parts of the kingdom to see their people and
give them instruction.

THE LINES
In the bottom line, SIX signifies:
*Contemplation like a child brings no reproach to the inferior
man; but for the superior man, humiliation.*
The ordinary people do not suffer from their lack of
understanding, but for the superior man such lack of
comprehension is shameful.

In the second line, SIX signifies:
*Contemplation through the crack of the door is sufficient
only for a housewife.*
A man (or a woman) who intends to engage in public
life must have an outlook broader than the purely
domestic.

In the third line, SIX signifies:
*Contemplation of ourselves determines the choice between
advance and retreat.*
One must strive to acquire objectivity by observing and
learning from one's emotions.

In the fourth line, SIX signifies:
*Contemplating the condition of the kingdom, he decides
to seek a place at court and flourishes.*
A man who understands how a kingdom is ruled
should be given a position of authority; but he will be
there more as a guest than as a minister.

In the fifth line, NINE signifies:
Contemplating his life, the superior man is without reproach.
The man in a position of authority should be ready to
examine his influence on others. If it is good, he will
enjoy the satisfaction of a blameless career.

In the sixth line, NINE signifies:
Contemplating himself, the superior man is without reproach.
The highest type of man has, after deepest self-
examination, excluded all selfish interests.

Biting Through

THE TRIGRAMS
ABOVE: Li fire, brightness
BELOW: Chen thunder and awakening
Shih Ho represents a mouth; the yang line in fourth place is something through which the teeth are biting. When bitten through, the mouth will be closed and obstacles cleared away.

THE JUDGMENT
Shih Ho signifies successful progress. It is advantageous to seek justice.

COMMENTARY
Union is brought about by biting through the intervening obstacles, and the hexagram indicates successful progress. Yang and yin lines are equally divided in the figure: thunder and movement are denoted by the lower trigram, brightness and intelligence by the upper. Thunder and lightning are the manifestation of the sudden release of tension in nature. A yin line occupies the fifth place, that of the ruler. Although this is not its proper position, it is advantageous for the processes of law.

THE IMAGE
Thunder and lightning are the symbol of biting through. The kings of old, therefore, framed their laws with care, making the punishment fit the crime.

THE LINES
In the bottom line, NINE signifies:
His feet are locked in the stocks, his toes are gone.
No reproach.
A justified punishment. Cutting off a man's toes was a Chinese punishment.

In the second line, SIX signifies:
Biting through tender meat, his nose is gone.
No reproach.
Cutting off a felon's nose was a punishment, and although this may be too severe a penalty, it is without blame.

In the third line, SIX signifies:
Biting through dried meat, he injures himself.
There is some humiliation, but no reproach.
The punishment is carried out by someone without sufficient authority and he injures himself. But he is performing his duty and will soon recover.

In the fourth line, NINE signifies:
Biting through dried gristle and bone, he receives the arrows demanded. It is advantageous to realise the difficulties, for perseverance brings good fortune.
In a civil court case, litigants would bring a bundle of arrows. By recognising the case's difficulties one can find the persistence to reach a just conclusion.

In the fifth line, SIX signifies:
Biting through dried lean meat, he receives the gold required. Aware of danger, he perseveres without reproach.
It was customary for the parties to deposit a sum of gold before a criminal hearing, yellow also being the colour of correctness in the middle way. If the judge is aware of the danger of making the wrong decision, his judgment will be just.

In the sixth line, NINE signifies:
His neck is locked in the wooden cangue, his ears are gone. Misfortune.
An instrument of punishment, the cangue was a wooden collar linking the shoulders and arms. The felon may have had his ears cut off.

22. 賁 Pi
Grace

THE TRIGRAMS
ABOVE: Ken mountain, stillness
BELOW: Li fire, brightness
A fire breaks out from the depths of the earth, blazing up to illuminate the heavenly heights of the mountain. The outer stillness of the mountain, lit from within by the inspiration of intelligence, is the symbol of grace.

THE JUDGMENT
Pi indicates that grace, impelled by brightness, should be given a free course. Even in minor matters it is advantageous to go forward.

COMMENTARY
The weak yin line rises between the two yang lines of the lower trigram, adorning them with its brilliance. The alteration of firmness and yielding is the pattern of heaven itself; by contemplating the patterns of heaven we begin to understand the changing seasons. As the earth adorns heaven, and heaven the earth, so the different levels of society adorn one another, and by observing them we can learn to live in grace.

THE IMAGE
Fire below the mountain is the symbol of grace. The superior man, observing this, throws light upon the processes of government, but does not dare to intervene in the processes of law.

THE LINES
In the bottom line, NINE signifies:
He adorns his feet, leaves his carriage,
And walks in grace.
He who begins in a subordinate position must learn to walk on his own two feet and makes sure that he is properly shod for his undertaking.

In the second line, SIX signifies:
He wears his beard with elegance.
A beard is the sign of sagacity, and he who wishes to associate with his elders should conform to their customs.

In the third line, NINE signifies:
Adorned, he glistens with grace.
Righteous perseverance brings good fortune.
Life is good, but such a state of affairs can only be maintained by perseverance in the true way.

In the fourth line, SIX signifies:
He is adorned, but only in white; a white horse with wings. One comes, not as a robber, but for a betrothal.
White signifies simplicity. He is unsure whether to pursue external brilliance, but the innocence of the horse returns him to simplicity.

In the fifth line, SIX signifies:
There is grace in hills and gardens. His silk girdle is thin and small. Disgrace, but in the end good fortune.
To be invited to walk in a great man's garden and then to appear poorly dressed, will bring humiliation. But it's a fault that will be forgiven.

In the sixth line, NINE signifies:
Nothing but grace in white. No reproach.
At the highest stage of development, true grace is to be found without adornment.

23. 剝 Po
Disintegration

THE TRIGRAMS

ABOVE: Ken mountain, stillness
BELOW: K'un Earth, the passive

Po means disintegration, breaking away from unnecessary encumbrances, and the first four lines of the hexagram symbolise a succession of losses which at first appear to be misfortunes, but which in the long run are resolved in the fifth line, leading to recognition of virtue in the sixth.

THE JUDGMENT

Disintegration. There is no direction in which to move with advantage.

COMMENTARY

In Po we see the weak yin lines threatening to shatter the last remaining yang lines and make it like themselves. Small men are increasing; the superior man, therefore, remains where he is and accepts the situation. He contemplates the ebb and flow of society about him, as the tides are moved by the heavenly bodies.

THE IMAGE

The mountain stands upon the earth, and symbolises disintegration: those above can only maintain their position by strengthening those below them.

THE LINES

In the bottom line, SIX signifies:
The leg of the bed is broken. Persistence brings disaster. Failure.
Inferior men undermine the superior man; even loyal men are threatened with misfortune. Accept the situation and await its outcome.

In the second line, SIX signifies:
The side of the bed is broken. Persistence brings disaster. Failure.
The superior man begins to mistrust even his friends. He must adjust himself to his conditions.

In the third line, SIX signifies:
He breaks with them. No reproach.
The individual severs all ties, relying only on his own integrity.

In the fourth line, SIX signifies:
The bed is overturned. His skin is split. Great misfortune.
Disaster has struck. The superior man is brought down, and his personal safety is threatened.

In the fifth line, SIX signifies:
A string of fishes, symbolising favour For the ladies of the court. Advantage in every way.
The empress leads her ladies in waiting like a line of fish. It is now good to move in any direction.

In the sixth line, NINE signifies:
The largest fruit, is uneaten on the tree. The superior man rides in his carriage. Inferior men throw down their houses.
Unplucked, the highest fruit will fall, planting a seed. The superior man has regained influence. Inferior men have brought destruction on themselves.

24. 復 Fu
The Turning Point

THE TRIGRAMS
ABOVE: K'un Earth, the passive
BELOW: Chen thunder and awakening
Fu is linked with the 11th month – the time of the winter solstice – and the turning point between years. It was believed that natural forces such as thunder rested in the earth in winter.

THE JUDGMENT
In Fu there is free going out and coming in, no-one to hinder. Friends arrive without blame, returning to their homes on the seventh day. Advantage in all directions.

COMMENTARY
This hexagram indicates success, because the strong yang line is rising from the bottom, returning to its natural starting point. Motion and acceptance of motion are combined in the two trigrams making up the hexagram; that is why there is going out and coming in without hindrance. This movement, with its return after seven days, is a natural motion in accord with the movements of heaven; and the very workings of heaven and earth are represented in the return to the turning point of the year.

THE IMAGE
Thunder within the earth is the very symbol of the turning point. So, at the time of the winter solstice, the kings closed the passes, so that merchants and strangers were unable to travel abroad, and the kings themselves did not pass through their dominions.

THE LINES
In the bottom line, NINE signifies:
Returning from a short distance: no regrets
And great good fortune.
He who turns back before he has gone too far, knowing the error he has made, is unblamed and brings good fortune on himself.

In the second line, SIX signifies:
Turning back with heaven's blessing. Good fortune.
All turning back requires a conscious decision and wins the approval of heaven.

In the third line. SIX signifies:
Turning back many times brings danger, but no reproach.
Those who lack constancy may find themselves lost in evil ways but, provided they recognise this danger, there is no blame.

In the fourth line, SIX signifies:
Walking with the others, but returning alone.
To be associated with companions, to realise that they are going in the wrong direction and to leave them.

In the fifth line, SIX signifies:
Turning back in nobleness, brings no remorse.
This represents a man of high principle who, recognising that he has gone astray, turns back whatever the cost.

In the sixth line, SIX signifies:
He turns back too late. Misfortune. Evil causes, evil effects. Armies sent into battle in this way are sure to suffer defeat. Disastrous to their emperor. Even for ten years there will be no redress.
When a man obstinately pursues the wrong path, there comes a point of no return. It will be a long time before he can attempt to right matters.

25. 无妄 Wu Wang
Innocence

THE TRIGRAMS
ABOVE: Ch'ien Heaven, the creative
BELOW: Chen thunder and awakening
Wang is the symbol of recklessness and insincerity; Wu Wang comprises meanings that are almost the opposite of this. But the innocence is so unsophisicated that it retains a trace of the unexpected.

THE JUDGMENT
Wu Wang indicates integrity, and resultant success. Persistence in righteousness brings its reward; but one who is not as he should be will suffer misfortune, and none of his undertakings will have a favourable outcome.

COMMENTARY
The strong first line becomes part of an outer trigram of three yang lines, forming Ch'ien, and enclosing an inner trigram, itself ruled by a strong line; the hexagram is full of power and movement. The fifth line is a yang line, in the place of the ruler, and the weak second line responds to it: he whose movement follows the laws of heaven will be innocent and without guile.

But incorrect action on the part of the subject will lead to errors that cannot easily be put right. In what direction should he move, even though he sincerely and innocently believes in everything he does? What can he achieve if it is not in accordance with the will of heaven?

THE IMAGE
The thunder rolls below the heavens, and all things find their true nature, free from all insincerity. So the kings, filled with virtue, made their laws according to the seasons and the ways of nature, bringing abundant nourishment to all mankind.

THE LINES
In the bottom line, NINE signifies:
Protected by his innocence and his in integrity
He achieves good fortune.
The noble impulses of the innocent are always good.

In the second line, SIX signifies:
Count not upon the harvest while still ploughing,
Nor upon the third year's crop before the first is in.
Count not your chickens before they are hatched.

In the third line, SIX signifies:
An unexpected misfortune: an untethered cow is
her master's loss, the gain of the passerby.
Carelessness or over confidence is followed
by calamity.

In the fourth line, NINE signifies:
Correct and resolute, he suffers no loss.
The open and candid man of integrity must know
when to resist the persuasion of others.

In the fifth line, NINE signifies:
Though he is ill, the fault is another's.
Without medicine, he will find joy in his recovery.
His difficulty is not of his own making. Let nature take
its course and the problem will solve itself.

In the sixth line, NINE signifies:
Unplanned, out of season, A journey can bring only
misfortune. The time is only favourable. For those with no
destination in mind.
When the time and conditions are not right, the wisest
course is to wait. Opposing oneself against fate can only
result in failure.

26. 大畜 Ta Ch'u
The Restraining Force

THE TRIGRAMS
ABOVE: Ken mountain, stillness
BELOW: Ch'ien Heaven, the creative
The creative power is subjugated to Ken, which imposes stillness. This contrasts with hexagram 9, Ch'u (the Power of the Weak), in which the creative power is tamed by gentleness. Here four strong lines are restrained by two weak lines, in the positions of both the prince and the minister.

THE JUDGMENT
Perseverance brings favourable results. Subsisting away from the home and family, without taking service at court, will bring good fortune. It is favourable to cross the great water.

COMMENTARY
Ta Ch'u symbolises strength and magnanimity, glory and honour, a daily renewal of character. The firm rises, paying respect to the worthy. Restraint in the exercise of power is praiseworthy. He who dines away from home is, by implication, entertaining other worthy people. Great and difficult undertakings, such as crossing the wide river or the sea, are successful because they accord with heaven's will.

THE IMAGE
Heaven beneath the mountain is the symbol of the restraining force of the great; at the same time we glimpse the sky among the mountain peaks. The superior man studies the sayings of antiquity and the deeds of heroes of the past, strengthening his innate virtue and learning to understand what is to come.

THE LINES
In the bottom line, NINE signifies:
Danger threatens. Avoid all action.
The man who wishes to go forward boldly, but who sees that circumstances oppose him, is wise not to attempt to overcome them.

In the second line, NINE signifies:
The springs of the wagon are broken.
There is no virtue in trying to fight the force which is holding one back.

In the third line, NINE signifies:
A good horse will gallop with the others. Go forward, aware of the dangers. Practise chariot driving and armed defence daily.
It is good to follow the example of a strong man, but it is important to have one's own definite goal.

In the fourth line, SIX signifies:
The headboard of a young bull. Great good fortune.
Deal with problems in advance. It was customary to attach a board to the head of young bull so that the horns would grow in an unharmful way.

In the fifth line, SIX signifies:
The tusks of a gelded boar. Good fortune.
Meet danger in advance. A castrated boar is less dangerous.

In the sixth line, NINE signifies:
Reaching command of heaven. Success.
There are no more obstructions: the wise man achieves everything he desires.

27. 頤 I
Nourishment

HE TRIGRAMS
BOVE: **Ken** mountain, stillness
ELOW: **Chen** thunder and awakening
he form of this hexagram is readily seen as a picture
f a mouth wide open to receive sustenance. The lower
ree lines represent nourishment of oneself, and the
pper trigram represents the nourishment of others,
articularly in a spiritual sense.

HE JUDGMENT
indicates that perseverance brings good fortune.
ay heed to those who nourish others, and observe
ow they seek to nourish themselves.

COMMENTARY
ake and give the right kind of nourishment, and good
ortune is assured. Observe the needs of others, both
hose who nourish themselves and those whom you
ould wish to nourish, but do not neglect your own
ustenance. As heaven and earth nourish all things, so
he wise man nourishes men of talent and virtue, and
hrough them reaches out to all the people, nourishing
hem both physically and spiritually.

THE IMAGE
Below the mountain the thunder rolls, the image
of nourishing. The superior man is careful of
verything that he says, and he observes due
moderation in his eating and drinking.

THE LINES
n the bottom line, NINE signifies:
*You let your magic tortoise go. Your mouth hangs open.
Misfortune.*
The tortoise was magical because it seemed to
ive off air. The man with his mouth agape has
abandoned self-reliance for envy or greed.

In the second line, SIX signifies:
*Turning from the path to seek nourishment in the
high hills.*
Having sought sustenance from those in high places,
the man succeeds only in bringing misfortune upon
himself.

In the third line, SIX signifies:
*Nourishment that nourishes not brings great misfortune.
Avoid such ways for ten years for there is no favourable
destination.*
Wandering from gratification to gratification brings no
satisfaction. Ten years is a complete cycle of time, and
signifies forever.

In the fourth line, SIX signifies:
*Good fortune comes from seeking nourishment in the high
hills. Staring about with hungry eyes like a tiger brings
no reproach.*
At first this seems to contradict the second line, but
the line now refers to a man who is searching for
others to help him attain his ideal.

In the fifth line, SIX signifies:
*Turning away from the path. Perseverance brings
good fortune. But success does not lie in crossing the
great water.*
Now is not the time for him to embark on any great
undertaking, because the man is still dependent upon
the assistance of others.

In the sixth line, NINE signifies:
*The fountain of nourishment. Watching for dangers
brings good fortune.*
A man who is now a great sage can, while taking note of
all the pitfalls and responsibilities that surround him,
undertake the most difficult labours.

28. 大過 Ta Kuo
Excess

THE TRIGRAMS
ABOVE: Tu a pool of water,
BELOW: Sun wind, gentleness, penetration
The four strong lines are held from without by two
weak lines. The hexagram is like a beam, thick
and heavy in the middle, but weak at its ends.

THE JUDGMENT
The weight is excessive. The ridgepole of the roof
sags and is near to breaking point. It is favourable
to have a destination.

COMMENTARY
This is a condition that cannot last: the weight of
the strong lines is too much for the weak ones.
The situation must be changed: an extraordinary
state of affairs demands extraordinary measures.
But although the tasks to be carried out are great,
nothing is to be gained by violent movement. The
gentle penetration of the wind is the example to
follow, and full consideration should be given to
the direction in which the desired change is to
be made.

THE IMAGE
The forest is submerged in the water, the pool
rises above it. The superior man, although
he stands alone, is free from fear; if he has to
withdraw from the world, he is undaunted.

THE LINES
In the bottom line, SIX signifies:
Spread white rushes upon the floor. No error.
Due caution is rewarded. If the roof is to be
lowered, then a mat of rushes should be spread to
take the weight. White rushes are the rarest.

In the second line, NINE signifies:
The withered tree sprouts from its roots. An old man
takes a young wife. Everything is favourable.
The old tree standing in the water puts forth new
shoots. In this situation of an old man taking a
young wife, all is well.

In the third line, NINE signifies:
The ridgepole sags. Misfortune.
A man who insists on driving ahead, taking
no advice from others but trying to force his
companions along, causes catastrophe.

In the fourth line, NINE signifies:
The ridgepole is shored up. Good fortune.
But if there is insincerity, humiliation.
A leader emerges, but if he does not work for the
good of all nothing but disgrace will ensue.

In the fifth line, NINE signifies:
The withered tree puts forth flowers. An old woman takes
a young husband. No blame. No praise.
An old woman may marry again, but she is barren
and no children will result. There is no evil in such
a situation, but equally no successful outcome.

In the sixth line, SIX signifies:
Wading through the water, it rose above his head.
Misfortune, but no blame.
The man goes forward courageously and although
he meets misfortune, the fault is not his own.

29. 坎 K'an
The Abyss

THE TRIGRAMS

ABOVE: **K'an** dangerous deep water
BELOW: **K'an** dangerous deep water

This is one of only eight hexagrams in which the trigram is doubled. In each trigram a strong yang line has plunged into the deep between two yin lines, and is closed in by them, as deep water lies in a ravine. The trigram K'an represents the soul of man enclosed within the body, the light of human reason locked up in the dark of animal instinct.

THE JUDGMENT

Abyss upon abyss, danger piled on danger. But if you are sincere there is success locked up within you, and whatever you undertake will be successful.

COMMENTARY

There is grave danger, but, as water flows without flooding over, so a man can cross the abyss without loss of confidence. Employing his reason he will succeed, and setting his eye upon a goal to be attained he will win respect and achieve results. The dangers sent from heaven none can escape, but earthly dangers are but mountains, rivers, hills and precipices. So, too, are the ominous means that are employed by kings and princes to protect their realms, both from without and within.

THE IMAGE

The water flows ever on and so reaches its destination: the image of the abyss upon the abyss. So the superior man walks in eternal virtue, instructing others in the conduct of affairs.

THE LINES

In the bottom line, SIX signifies:
Abyss upon abyss. He falls into the depths. Misfortune.
A man can become hardened to danger and turn to evil ways. He is bound to be caught.

In the second line, NINE signifies:
The abyss is dangerous and deep. Taking small steps, he only slowly climbs out.
It is best to overcome dangers by gradual means.

In the third line, SIX signifies:
Forward and backward, abyss beneath abyss.
He falls deeper into the pit unable to help himself.
Wasting one's energies on fruitless attempts, one finds oneself in greater danger.

In the fourth line, SIX signifies:
A flagon of wine and with it a bowl of rice, handed in through a hole in the rock. There is certainly no blame.
Rough and ready help is at hand, but although the fault is not one's own, little can be done about it.

In the fifth line, NINE signifies:
The water does not overflow the abyss, rising only to the brim. There is no blame.
The way out of danger is to follow the line of least resistance, just as water flows out of the ravine. In great danger it is enough to escape by any means.

In the sixth line, SIX signifies:
Bound with black ropes, hedged in by thorns, for three years he cannot find the way. Great misfortune.
Although the man's perilous situation will persist, it will not last forever and he can plan for his release.

Flaming Beauty

THE TRIGRAMS
ABOVE: Li fire, Brightness, beauty
BELOW: Li fire, Brightness, beauty
Another doubled hexagram. The trigram Li means both 'clinging' and 'brightness', as the flame burns bright and is defined by the object on which it burns.

THE JUDGMENT
Li is the clinging flame. Persistence brings great good fortune. Nurturing cows brings rewards and blessings.

COMMENTARY
The sun and moon depend from heaven, as living things depend upon earth. Clear bright consciousness of what is right results in the transforming and perfecting of all things under heaven. The weak yin lines in the second and fifth positions between the strong yang lines indicate success and the fact that docility like that of a cow will lead to good fortune.

THE IMAGE
Fire rises in two tongues of flaming beauty. Likewise the wise man sheds his light over every quarter of the earth.

THE LINES
In the bottom line, NINE signifies:
First light: tracks run in all directions. But approaching with respectful steps, he suffers no blame.
Still sleepy in the morning, people may set off in the wrong direction, but one who remains calm can set about his tasks without confusion.

In the second line, SIX signifies:
Bright yellow sunlight. Great good fortune.
It is now full daylight. Yellow is the colour of moderation. The middle way, the golden mean, brings success.

In the third line, NINE signifies:
In the light of the setting sun, he does not strike his ch'ing and sing, but mourns his lost youth. Misfortune.
At the end of the day, the man who does not celebrate the pleasure of his life, and what has yet to come, will bring only sadness upon himself.

In the fourth line, NINE signifies:
It comes so suddenly. Flames up, dies, and is cast away.
A man who rises suddenly to success will as suddenly vanish again from view.

In the fifth line, SIX signifies:
His tears flow in torrents, he groans in sorrow. Good fortune.
Having reaching the high point of his life, the man understands the vanity of all things and regrets his past wrongs.

In the sixth line, NINE signifies:
The king sends him forth, to punish and set things right. Victorious, he kills the rebel leader, but takes his followers captive. No reproach.
Punishment should not be distributed indiscriminately.

31.咸 Hsien
Influence

THE TRIGRAMS
ABOVE: Tui a pool of water, joy
BELOW: Ken mountain, stillness
Ken, the lower trigram, represents the youngest son; Tui, the upper, represents the youngest daughter. Thus this hexagram signifies the persuasive influence that exists between the sexes, representing wooing and marriage.

THE JUDGMENT
Influence, attraction, success. Righteous perseverance furthers one's desires. Taking a maiden for a wife brings good fortune.

COMMENTARY
The yielding trigram Tui is above, the firm trigram Ken is below. Although they are opposite in nature, their mutual attraction draws them together. In many of the most auspicious of Taoist positions for sexual intercourse the man is below the woman. All nature owes its existence to the influence of earth upon heaven, and heaven upon earth. In the same way, the wise man exerts his influence upon men's hearts, observing what causes them pleasure and what causes pain, and bringing the whole world to peace.

THE IMAGE
The lake is high upon the mountain. So the superior man welcomes those who approach him, humbly and without selfishness.

THE LINES
In the bottom line, SIX signifies:
He feels the influence in his big toe.
Even before a man begins to move, he reveals his activity in a flexing of his toes. As long as it is not visible, it has no importance to others.

In the second line, SIX signifies:
The influence shows itself in the legs. Misfortune.
It is better not to venture forth.
An ill conceived movement of the legs may result in a fall. Better to remain where one is until the persuasive influence is understood.

In the third line, NINE signifies:
He feels the influence in his loins.
Clinging to his wife in this way is shameful.
A man who follows the dictates of his heart or his animal instincts rather than of his head.

In the fourth line, NINE signifies:
Righteous perseverance brings good fortune.
There are no regrets. But when a man is agitated in mind, his thoughts flying to and fro, only his closest friends will be influenced by him.
The man who acts without consideration will find it difficult to persuade more than his nearest companions to follow him.

In the fifth line, NINE signifies:
The influence is felt in the nape of the neck.
No regrets.
Resolution shows itself in a stiffening of the back and neck. But even though the man feels no remorse, he may have difficulty persuading others.

In the sixth line, SIX signifies:
The influence shows itself in the jaws and tongue.
Trying to persuade others by talk alone is a superficial way of doing things.

<h2>32. 恆 Heng</h2>

Endurance

THE TRIGRAMS

ABOVE: Chen thunder and awakening
BELOW: Sun wind, gentleness, penetration

This hexagram, with the strong trigram Chen above the weak trigram Sun, is the exact inverse of Hsien, the preceding hexagram, and represents the bonds of an enduring marriage.

THE JUDGMENT

Endurance signifies steady progress, with success and freedom from error. Righteous persistence brings its reward; and it is certainly favourable to have a destination in view.

COMMENTARY

Thunder and wind work together, representing gentleness combined with arousal. The interplay of strong and weak lines makes for endurance, and success, freedom from error and the rewards of righteous persistence all indicate that the established way can be pursued for a long time; for the way, as it is followed by heaven and earth, sun and moon, endures for ever, and the four seasons, continuing their ceaseless cycle of transformation, extend their influence for eternity. The wise man keeps steadfastly to his chosen path, succeeding in transforming all things under heaven and rendering them perfect. The true nature of everything in heaven and earth can be discovered in contemplating what it is that makes them endure.

THE IMAGE

Thunder and wind, the one influencing the other, are the image of endurance. The superior man stands firm, his direction unaltered.

THE LINES

In the bottom line, SIX signifies:
Lasting success is not attained hastily by digging a burrow for oneself. Persistence in this course brings misfortune, for one is without destination.
The man who attempts to establish a lasting position by entrenching himself in his present circumstances shows no thought for the future.

In the second line, NINE signifies:
There are no regrets.
The man who realises that he is not yet ready, who does not attempt anything beyond his present powers, will have no regrets.

In the third line, NINE signifies:
Lacking persistence in his virtuous conduct, he meets with disgrace and lasting humiliation.
A man who changes with the wind will be deserted by friends and will end his life in shame.

In the fourth line, NINE signifies:
There is no quarry in the field.
Persistence itself is not enough. A man who takes his bow to the field, hunting where there is no game to be shot at, is foolish.

In the fifth line, SIX signifies:
Obstinate constancy is favourable for a woman, but not for a man.
Adhering blindly to tradition and conformity is appropriate for a wife, but a man can lose sight of his ultimate destination.

In the sixth line, SIX signifies:
Persisting in ceaseless activity brings misfortune.
Insisting upon immediate action will not give a man time to avoid errors.

33. 遯 Tun

Withdrawal

THE TRIGRAMS
ABOVE: Ch'ien Heaven, the creative
BELOW: Ken mountain, stillness
The dark power of Ken rises from below, and the spiritual light retreats before it to safety. This hexagram is associated with the sixth month of the year, in which the power of the sun begins to decline. Retreat is not a matter to be decided wilfully by man, but a natural process, and withdrawal in these circumstances is proper.

THE JUDGMENT
Withdrawal means success. Persistence in small matters is nevertheless to one's advantage.

COMMENTARY
In certain situations a retreat is in effect an advance. A strong yang line is in the fifth place, the place of the ruler, and all the other lines respond to it: all actions take place in accordance with the times. As young plants grow when properly watered, so persistence in small matters brings advantage. A withdrawal at the proper time signifies success.

THE IMAGE
The mountain stands below heaven. The superior man, keeping his distance from men of inferior character, is not angry but dignified.

THE LINES
In the bottom line, SIX signifies:
Withdrawing with the rearguard. This is dangerous.
The rearguard of a retreating army is designed for sacrifice. There is no time, in the disorder of a retreat, to seek out a direction of one's own.

In the second line, SIX signifies:
He binds him with yellow rawhide thongs.
None can untie them.
With a powerful will, the inferior man is tightly bound to the superior, so that he cannot be shaken loose and can achieve his goal.

In the third line, NINE signifies:
Delay in withdrawal is frightening and dangerous.
But retaining the servants and concubines
Brings good fortune.
The most obvious course is to abandon the retainers who cause delay, but the superior man leads them out of danger.

In the fourth line, NINE signifies:
Choosing withdrawal, the superior man benefits,
But the inferior man is destroyed.
The man who makes a calculated retreat from a dangerous situation, not allowing himself to be burdened with an inferior, escapes.

In the fifth line, NINE signifies:
Withdrawal by agreement. Perseverance brings
good fortune.
When the time is right for retreat, the wise man recognises it, and there is no need for discussion. But he must still adhere to his decision.

In the sixth line, NINE signifies:
Happy withdrawal. Everything is favourable.
The superior man has reached a spiritual state free from doubt, and there are now no obstacles to his retiring from the world into contemplation.

34. 大 壯 Ta Chuang
Strength of Greatness

THE TRIGRAMS

ABOVE: Chen thunder and awakening
BELOW: Ch'ien Heaven, the creative

The four strong yang lines have entered from below and are ascending; the combination of the strength of Ch'ien with the powerful movement of Chen is what gives meaning to the name of this hexagram. In appearance it is reminiscent of the horned head of the goat, an animal renowned for rapid, powerful movement. The hexagram is also linked with the second month of the Chinese year, the time when everything is springing to life.

THE JUDGMENT

Ta Chuang is the strength of the great. Perseverance in a course of righteousness brings reward.

COMMENTARY

The strength of righteousness and greatness combined brings full understanding of the inner nature of everything in heaven and on earth. The lower trigram, signifying strength, controls the upper, which signifies movement, and from this results great vigour. Righteous persistence is duly rewarded because, in the context of this hexagram, what is great and what is right are synonymous.

THE IMAGE

Thunder above the heavens is the image of the strength of greatness. The superior man does not lead a path that is not in accord with established order.

THE LINES

In the bottom line, NINE signifies:
Strength in the toes. But going forward brings misfortune, this is certainly true. Have confidence.
Trying to advance by strength (the feet are furthest from the brain) without intelligence will lead to disaster.

In the second line, NINE signifies:
Righteous persistence brings good fortune.
There are now opportunities for advancement, but it is wise still not to plunge ahead.

In the third line, NINE signifies:
The inferior man exploits his strength, but the superior man is restrained, for persistence is dangerous: the goat butts obstinately against the hedge and his horns are caught.
The inferior man glories in and abuses power, but the wise man will limit his power when there is no purpose in an empty display of strength.

In the fourth line, NINE signifies:
Righteous persistence brings good fortune, regrets vanish. The hedge falls apart, the goat frees himself.
Obstacles are best overcome by calm and intelligent perseverance.

In the fifth line, SIX signifies:
The goat is lost too easily, but there is no cause for regret.
The situation has been resolved, perhaps too easily. Nevertheless, abandoning one's obstinate position at this point will bring no misfortune.

In the sixth line, SIX signifies:
The goat butts obstinately against the hedge, there is no advantage in going on, but taking due note of the mistake, brings good fortune.
The more one struggles, the more one is ensnared. But by coming to an understanding of the obstacle one can find the solution.

35. 晉 Chin
Progress

THE TRIGRAMS
ABOVE: Li fire, brightness, beauty
BELOW: K'un Earth, the passive
The hexagram represents the sun rising over the earth, a symbol of steady progress.

THE JUDGMENT
The great prince is honoured with many horses, and in a single day the emperor grants him three audiences.

COMMENTARY
Chin means progress. The combination of the passive trigram K'un with the beauty of Li represents the earth radiant with bright light. The weak yin lines ascend to the fifth and ruling line of the hexagram, signifying a great prince, splendid steeds, and royal favour.

The effect of progress comes from the prince, a man subservient to his emperor but at the same time a leader of others. He does not abuse his influence, but dedicates it to the service of his ruler who, enlightened and free from jealousy, showers favours upon him.

THE IMAGE
Chin is the image of progress, the sun rising above the earth. The superior man reflects in himself the brightness of heavenly virtue.

THE LINES
In the bottom line, SIX signifies:
Going forward, then hindered; but persistence brings good fortune. He meets lack of confidence with tranquillity. No error.
One may be brought to a halt by influences beyond one's control. One should remain cheerfully untroubled by the delay.

In the second line, SIX signifies:
Progress in sorrow. Persistence brings good fortune. And great happiness comes from the honoured grandmother.
Receiving no recognition, the progress causes sorrow. But persevere, because in time someone will give instruction.

In the third line, SIX signifies:
All are in accord. Sorrow vanishes.
Aware of the support of others, one realises one is making true progress.

In the fourth line, NINE signifies:
Making progress like a squirrel. Persistence is dangerous.
Like a squirrel forgetting where its food is buried, a man can amass great possessions but seldom reaches his goal and often loses everything.

In the fifth line, SIX signifies:
All sorrow vanishes. Care not for loss or gain. It is advantageous to have a destination. All things are favourable.
A man in an important position should remain impassive and not regret any past mistakes. He should be positive that his ventures will succeed.

In the sixth line, NINE signifies:
He butts onward with lowered horns Only to subdue his own people. Consciousness of his danger brings no blame. But persistence results in humiliation.
Progressing by attack is only permissible when correcting the mistakes of one's followers. One who is aware of danger is able to avoid mistakes.

Sinking Light

THE TRIGRAMS
ABOVE: K'un Earth, the passive
BELOW: Li fire, brightness, beauty
The sun has sunk beneath the earth: the name of the hexagram, Ming I, literally means 'wounding of the bright'. This hexagram comprises not only a transposition of the trigrams of the previous hexagram, but is its inversion. In Chin, a wise man, assisted by competent helpers, made steady progress; in Ming I, the wise man is in peril from a malevolent man in authority.

THE JUDGMENT
The light is sinking. Righteous persistence in the face of adversity brings advancement.

COMMENTARY
As the sun declines into the earth, so its light is extinguished. Meet adversity like King Wen, attiring your inner self in refinement and intelligence, displaying gentleness and compliance in your outward behaviour. Determined to triumph over all difficulties, hide your light under a bushel. Be like Prince Chi who, with his troubles locked within his heart, fixed his whole being upon righteousness with rigid determination.

THE IMAGE
The light sinks into the earth, the image of Ming I. The superior man, walking among the people, keeps his light hidden. But still it shines.

THE LINES
In the bottom line, NINE signifies:
The light sinks as he flies through the sky, his wings droop. For three days, busy about his occasions, the superior man goes without food or rest. Though his lord whispers about it, he has a goal in view.
One who has a true goal will be honoured, even though those above him criticised him for persistence.

In the second line, SIX signifies:
The light sinks. Wounded in the thigh, he saves himself by the strength of a horse. And brings assistance. Good fortune.
Although the superior man conceals his light, he is harmed by someone in authority. But striving, he brings relief to the distress of others in a similar plight.

In the third line, NINE signifies:
The light sinks as he searches in the south and captures the prince of darkness. But foolish persistence must be avoided.
By good chance, the wise man vanquishes his enemy. But he showed excessive zeal that amounted almost to madness.

In the fourth line, SIX signifies:
Leaving his gate and courtyard, he thrusts into the left of the belly and exposes the heart of the prince of darkness.
As he sets out from his place of safety, the wise man has exposed the nature of his adversary. But he realises that the evil is too great and has to withdraw.

In the fifth line, SIX signifies:
The light sinks. As it sank for Prince Chi. But righteous persistence is rewarded.
Prince Chi feigned insanity and was treated as little more than a slave. But he still believed that the true light can never be extinguished.

In the sixth line, SIX signifies:
No light in the darkness. After, ascending to the heavens, he plunged into the depths of earth.
The prince of darkness is triumphant. But the darkness brings its own destruction, and in the end evil will be overcome.

37. 家人 Chia Jen
The Family

THE TRIGRAMS
ABOVE: Sun wind, gentleness, penetration
BELOW: Li fire, brightness, beauty
This hexagram represents the strength of the family. The strong yang line at the top is the father, the strong bottom line the son. The strong line in the fifth place may also represent the father, the weak yin line in second place the wife: alternatively, the strong lines in fifth and third place are two brothers, the weak second and fourth lines their wives. Each individual line possesses the character in accordance with its position.

THE JUDGMENT
It is the woman's persistence that brings good fortune. Women who cast this hexagram should take it as a favourable omen, but for men it does not have a successful significance.

COMMENTARY
It is the place of women to keep within; men stand without. Keeping to their appointed places, men and women act in accordance with the laws of heaven; when the family is in order, then all the social relationships of mankind are also in order. When father, mother, sons and brothers take their proper positions within the structure of the family, when husbands play their proper part and wives are truly wifely, all is well.

THE IMAGE
The wind rises from the fire. The words of the superior man are full of meaning, his life is constant and endures.

THE LINES
In the bottom line, NINE signifies:
The family circle is closed and in good order.
Regret vanishes.
Every family member knows his place. If a child is allowed to exercise his whims, he and his parents will eventually regret the indulgence.

In the second line, SIX signifies:
She should not indulge her whims but attend to the needs of the household. Persistence brings good fortune.
One in service to a single household or to the state should not follow his selfish desires but devote himself to his duties.

In the third line, NINE signifies:
When there are quarrels in the family, too much strictness brings regret, but nevertheless good fortune. When women and children mock, disgrace.
Discipline tempered with tenderness is the best means of preserving concord. Nevertheless, strictness is preferred to indulgence.

In the fourth line, SIX signifies:
She is the treasure of the house. Great good fortune.
Any woman of the house who nourishes the family and supervises its economy.

In the fifth line, NINE signifies:
He is a king in his own house. Fear not; good fortune.
When a husband governs his family as a king governs his kingdom, all is well. Ruling justly, he brings prosperity to all.

In the sixth line, NINE signifies:
His sincerity and confidence bring him honour.
Good fortune in the end.
The man who subjects his actions to constant self-examination will bring good fortune to himself and to all his dependants.

Opposites

THE TRIGRAMS

ABOVE: Lui fire, brightness, beauty
BELOW: Tui a pool of water, joy

Li, the flame, burns upward, while Tui, the pool of water, soaks downward – two movements that are opposites. Moreover, Li represents the second daughter and Tui the youngest daughter: though they may live in the same house their attentions are directed at two different men, and therefore their desires run in opposite directions.

THE JUDGMENT

Opposites – but in small matters, good fortune.

COMMENTARY

Fire moves upward, water moves downward, like two women under one roof whose wills do not accord. But if joy is joined to beauty, there is radiance. The weak yin lines ascend, responding to the strong yang lines and indicating good fortune in minor matters. For, although heaven and earth may be separate and apart, they work towards the same end; men and women are opposite, but they desire union; all things are individual, but each accomplishes its purpose in accordance with its kind.

THE IMAGE

Fire above, and the pool below: the image of K'uei. The superior man remains himself, even in the midst of the crowd.

THE LINES

In the bottom line, NINE signifies:
There are no regrets. He loses his horse, but should not run after it. For it will return of itself. Meeting with evil men, he avoids condemnation.
It is impossible to dismiss evil men forcibly, or to ignore them, and so one should endure their company until they leave of their own accord.

In the second line, NINE signifies:
He meets his lord in a narrow street. No blame.
An accidental encounter between two people not on good terms. With no way they can avoid one another, friendly relations are re-established.

In the third line, SIX signifies:
He sees his wagon halted, the oxen reined back. His hair and his nose are cut off. An ominous beginning but an auspicious end.
Everything is going wrong. K'uei is different by only the second line from hexagram 21 (Shih Ho biting through).

In the fourth line, NINE signifies:
Solitary and estranged, one meets a like-minded person with whom to live in confidence. There is danger, but no mistake.
Someone who seems to share one's isolation can assume an exaggerated significance. But if one is alert, it can be turned to the best advantage.

In the fifth line, SIX signifies:
Regrets vanish. He cleaves to his companion as if he bit through the thin skin. Going forward.
At first, one does not recognise the true friend; then it is as if a veil had been torn away.

In the sixth line, NINE signifies:
Wandering solitary and estranged, he sees a pig caked with mud, a wagonload of devils. First he draws his bow against them, then lays it aside; for this is no assailant but a close relative. He goes forward in soft rain; good fortune comes.
As the soft rain of summer cleans dirt and dust from everything, so one's doubts are swept away and one advances toward a successful outcome.

Obstacles

THE TRIGRAMS
ABOVE: K'an water, dangerous pit
BELOW: Ken mountain, stillness
The hexagram represents a perilous abyss in front, a precipitous mountain behind. Whichever way one turns, one's path is beset with obstacles.

THE JUDGMENT
There is advantage to the south and west; obstacles to the north and east. It is advantageous to see and meet a great man. Righteous persistence brings good fortune.

COMMENTARY
Chien denotes difficulty, because danger lies in front of one. Wisdom lies in perceiving the danger and successfully avoiding it: the southwest is the direction of retreat, and that way leads to the middle course, but the northeast is the direction of advance, and nothing favourable lies that way. The strong yang line in the fifth position indicates that righteous persistence will be of great value to the community or the state; visiting a great man is bound to result in significant achievements.

THE IMAGE
Water upon the mountain, the image of Chien. So the superior man turns back in order to examine himself and cultivate his virtue.

THE LINES
In the bottom line, SIX signifies:
Going forward means obstacles, standing still earns praise.
Encountering obstacles, one should not attempt to go forward, but consider the situation.

In the second line, SIX signifies:
The servant of the king encounters obstacle after obstacle, but the fault is not his.
This is the path of duty: when a man must continue to struggle in the service of others, then he should not be reproached.

In the third line, NINE signifies:
Going forward leads only to obstacles and he turns back.
It would be foolish to push forward into danger, and if a man turns back he will be welcomed by his kin.

In the fourth line, SIX signifies:
Going forward leads to obstacles. Remaining still he allies himself with those who are on their way.
In this situation a man cannot overcome obstacles by himself; he must wait until others join him.

In the fifth line, NINE signifies:
He struggles against all obstacles, but friends are coming to help him.
The man is called to help. Even though the dangers are too great for him, his example attracts others to the cause.

In the sixth line, SIX signifies:
Going forward leads to obstacles, remaining still brings great good fortune. Now is the time to see the great man.
The sage may move spiritually but his practical nature draws him back to the world, where his teaching brings him and others good fortune.

40. 解 Hsieh
Deliverance

THE TRIGRAMS
ABOVE: Che thunder and awakening
BELOW: K'an water, dangerous pit
Hsieh represents deliverance from the dangers of Chien, the previous hexagram. The obstacles have been removed, troubles are resolved. However, deliverance is only beginning, and the lines of the hexagram represent its progressive stages.

THE JUDGMENT
There is advantage to the south and west. Those who have no good reason to go forward will gain good fortune by turning back. Those who have a destination in view should hasten forward to be sure of success.

COMMENTARY
Hsieh represents deliverance from danger by activity. South and west are favourable, because those who go in this direction, that of retreat, will be loved by all; and turning back brings good fortune and makes it possible to follow the middle way. But those with a good reason to go forward should hurry on their way. When heaven and earth are released from the clutch of winter through thunder and rain, the buds of fruit trees and every sort of plant burst open. Great indeed are events in the time of Hsieh!

THE IMAGE
Thunder and rain begin, the image of deliverance. The superior man forgives mistakes and pardons crimes.

THE LINES
In the bottom line, SIX signifies:
No error!
With the obstacles removed, there is nothing to be done except rest and be thankful.

In the second line, NINE signifies:
Taking the yellow arrow, he kills three foxes in the field.
Righteous persistence brings success.
Yellow is the colour of moderation and honour; the fox is sly. But commentators disagree on the text: does the hunter kill three foxes with a single arrow or is he rewarded with the arrow?

In the third line, SIX signifies:
Carrying his baggage on his back, yet riding in a carriage, he tempts robbers to attack him.
Persistence in this course brings nothing but shame.
As Confucius says: 'A man who is insolent toward those above him and unyielding to those below him, tempts robbers to plot an attack on him.'

In the fourth line, NINE signifies:
Release yourself with your toe. Then friends will come, in whom you can put your trust.
Deliverance is difficult: as if a man is trying to untie himself with his toes. He has encumbered himself with inferior people and must break free.

In the fifth line, SIX signifies:
The superior man can deliver himself and enjoys good fortune. Proving his worthiness to inferior men.
The inferior are difficult to be rid of; the superior man must first break with them in his mind and only then will they accept his decision and let go.

In the sixth line, SIX signifies:
The prince draws his bow and slays the falcon on the high wall. Everything is favourable.
Still hindered from deliverance by an inferior in a position of importance, the superior man must prepare for his release and act with resolve.

41. 損 Sun
Decrease

THE TRIGRAMS
ABOVE: Ken mountain, stillness
BELOW: Tui a pool of water, joy
This hexagram is regarded as having been formed by a change in hexagram 11 (T'ai, Peace). The strong yang line in the third place is replaced by the weak yin line from the top; so that what is below has been decreased to the advantage of what is above. It is as if the foundations of a building had been weakened while the upper walls were strengthened.

THE JUDGMENT
One who effects decrease with sincerity will bring about great good fortune without blame. Righteous persistence is correct, and there is advantage in every move made towards a destination. If there is doubt about how to proceed, two small bowls are sufficient for the sacrifice.

COMMENTARY
There is loss below, but gain above, and the way leads ever upwards. The use of two small bowls means that one should use whatever comes to hand. At times it is right to decrease the strong and increase the weak. Decrease and increase, filling and emptying – there is an appointed time for each.

THE IMAGE
The lake lies at the foot of the mountain, the image of Sun. The superior man controls his anger and suppresses his desires.

THE LINES
In the bottom line, NINE signifies:
When work is done, hurry away: this is not wrong.
It is kind to help others, but how much more can a man take on and will it really be of assistance?

In the second line, NINE signifies:
Righteous persistence brings reward. But going forward brings misfortune. One can bring increase to others without decreasing oneself.
Someone who sacrifices his principles at the insistence of another diminishes not only himself.

In the third line, SIX signifies:
If three set out together, one is lost by the way. But a man going forth alone finds company.
Among three, jealousy is bound to arise. But a man who sets out on his own will find a partner.

In the fourth line, SIX signifies:
Decreasing his faults, he finds another hurrying to rejoice. No blame.
When a man recognises his shortcomings, his friends will flock around him.

In the fifth line, SIX signifies:
He is increased by many – ten pair or more – of tortoise shells. Great good fortune.
Tortoise shells were used in divination. To someone destined for good fortune, it will come without fail.

In the sixth line, NINE signifies:
Increasing without reducing others, he is without blame. Righteous persistence brings good fortune. It is favourable to have a destination. He hires servants but has no family or home.
The successful man can enlist the help of others, butt his actions will be devoted to public service not his private life and will be for the good of all.

Increase

THE TRIGRAMS
ABOVE: Sun wind, gentleness, penetration
BELOW: Che thunder and awakening
This hexagram represents increase because it is a development from hexagram 12 (P'i, Stagnation): the strong yang line of the upper trigram has sunk to the bottom, and is rising through the lower trigram. This expresses the fundamental conception that to rule truly is to serve.

THE JUDGMENT
It is favourable to have a destination; now is the time to cross the great water.

COMMENTARY
There is loss above and gain below, and the joy of the people is boundless, because when those placed above behave virtuously and without pride towards those below them their ways are brilliantly illuminated. It is favourable to have a destination, because the way is straight and lies in the middle, leading to unexpected good fortune. Finding a wooden bridge or a boat, you may cross the great water. Increase comes at once and constantly, every day brings unhindered progress. Heaven dispenses its blessings and earth brings forth its fruits. At the appointed time, increase is everywhere.

THE IMAGE
Wind and thunder, the image of I. The superior man, seeing what is good, imitates it; recognising his faults, he corrects them.

THE LINES
In the bottom line, NINE signifies:
Now is the time for great undertakings. Great good fortune. No blame.
He who is favoured with great ability must use it to achieve something and those below him will help.

In the second line, SIX signifies:
There is someone who indeed increases him. With many pair of tortoise shells and will not accept refusal. Persistence brings good fortune. The king presents his offerings to the lord of heaven. Good fortune.
When destiny smiles on a man, everything he strives for will come to him. But only a virtuous man will enjoy such a fate.

In the third line, SIX signifies:
He is increased by evil means, but, acting in all sincerity, he is not to blame. Walking confidently in the centre, bearing his jade seal of office, he reports to his prince.
The man who walks the middle way will prosper even in the midst of adversity. The jade seal that he carries is the symbol of his faithfulness.

In the fourth line, SIX signifies:
Walking in the centre, he advises the prince and is followed. He is the man to be used in moving the place of government.
When the capital is moved (as it was during the Shang Dynasty (16–11th century BCE), great trust must be placed in the man responsible.

In the fifth line, NINE signifies:
Be sincere and kind, ask no questions and great good fortune will result. All will recognise your confidence and virtue.
The ruler bestows good things on his people without demanding their allegiance.

In the sixth line, NINE signifies:
He brought increase to no-one and someone sought to strike him. He is not constant in his heart. Misfortune.
Those in high places who neglect those below them will find themselves isolated and perhaps even attacked by those they have abandoned.

43. 夬 Kuai
Resolution

THE TRIGRAMS
ABOVE: Tui a pool of water, joy
BELOW: Ch'ien Heaven, the creative
Ch'ien represents the father, and Tui the youngest
daughter; the strong yang lines are rising upwards
through the hexagram, and cannot be restrained
by the weak yin line at the top. The result will be a
breakthrough, like a cloudburst or a river bursting
its banks. Kuai is associated with the third month
of the year, when there are frequent rainstorms.

THE JUDGMENT
Everything should be reported in full at the king's
court, even though frankness is dangerous. When
reporting to one's own city, it is not proper to be
armed. It is good to have a destination in view.

COMMENTARY
Kuai is the symbol of displacing with
determination, because the strong resolve the
affairs of the weak; strength is combined with
cheerfulness and determination with placidity.
Reporting – possibly the guilt of a criminal – at the
king's court is indicated by the single weak line
above the five strong lines. The importance of a
known destination is also indicated by the way
in which the movement of these strong lines is
brought to an end.

THE IMAGE
The lake has risen above the heavens, the image of
Kuai. The superior man, accordingly, bestows his
gifts upon those below him; he does not rest upon
his virtues.

THE LINES
In the bottom line, NINE signifies:
Mighty and proud in his strength, he advances his feet.
But he is unequal to the task and suffers humiliation.
Similar to the bottom line of hexagram 34: an
attempt to go forward by brute strength without
considering the means or the outcome.

In the second line, NINE signifies:
Shouts in the night. But he who is forearmed is
forewarned and has no fear.
The superior man is always on his guard.

In the third line, NINE signifies:
Setting the jaw and advancing straight forward
brings misfortune. The superior man determines on
interception. Walking alone in the rain, he is spattered
with mud and his friends murmur against him.
No blame.
The wise man has to risk being misjudged by
others but his virtue will be recognised in
the end.

In the fourth line, NINE signifies:
His haunches are flayed and he walks with difficulty.
Letting himself be led like a sheep, he could put an
end to his pain. But though he hears this advice, he
believes it not.
Obstinacy deafens a man to all good counsel.

In the fifth line, NINE signifies:
Like a bed of weeds, tenacious but shallow-rooted,
inferior men cling to the earth. The superior man,
determined to uproot them, treads the middle way and
suffers no reproach.
The inferior man in a high position holds
desperately to his place and it takes dangerous
determination to remove him.

In the sixth line, SIX signifies:
There is no warning. The end is misfortune.
When victory appears to be in one's grasp,
a moment of inattention can bring disaster.

44. 姤 Kou
Coming Together

THE TRIGRAMS

ABOVE: Ch'ien Heaven, the creative
BELOW: Sun wind, gentleness, penetration
This hexagram is linked with the fifth month, the
time of the summer solstice, when the first whisper
of the darkness of the coming winter is heard.
This is the weak yin line, driven from the top of
the preceding hexagram, furtively reappearing
at the bottom: it represents the female principle
advancing to meet the male. Although it signifies
the pleasure of sexual intercourse, it also contains
elements of danger.

THE JUDGMENT
Coming together, meaning the woman is in power. A
marriage in such circumstances would be unfavourable.

COMMENTARY
The yielding confronts the firm. A marriage with
such a woman would not last long. Nevertheless,
it is from such an intercourse that heaven and
earth give birth to all things, and when strength is
properly controlled and correctly used, everything
in the world goes well. And great indeed is the
importance of what is done at the right time
indicated by Kou.

THE IMAGE
The wind is below the heavens, the image of
Kou. Accordingly, the prince gives out his orders,
proclaiming them to the four quarters of the kingdom.

THE LINES
In the bottom line, SIX signifies:
*The wheel is checked with a brake of bronze; righteous
persistence brings good fortune. It is not fortunate to have a
destination. A lean pig still struggles.*
A bad influence must be constantly checked. A pig
should be fat so it must not be allowed to run about.

In the second line, NINE signifies:
*The fish is in the bag. No error. But it is not for
the guests.*
The fish is a wily, untrustworthy influence
that must be kept confined.

In the third line, NINE signifies:
*His haunches are flayed and he walks with difficulty.
Mindful of his danger, he makes no great mistake.*
Going forward obstinately, even though one is
suffering, is unwise. But the man who knows what
he is doing will suffer no misfortune.

In the fourth line, NINE signifies:
There is no fish in the bag. Misfortune.
It is necessary to make use of inferior people in
furthering one's aims. The man who does not do
so will lose them through his indifference.

In the fifth line, NINE signifies:
*The medlar leaves shade the melon, hiding its beauty.
Then it drops as if from heaven.*
Shaded, the melon does not ripen too quickly – the
superior man protects those below him but does
not let them know they are in his co
ntrol.

In the sixth line, NINE signifies:
He meets them with his horns. Regrets, but no blame.
A man who holds himself aloof will be reproached,
but he does not care about his contemporaries'
opinions.

Congregation

THE TRIGRAMS
ABOVE: Tui a pool of water, joy
BELOW: K'un Earth, the passive
Ts'ui is related to hexagram 8 (Pi, Seeking Unity).
In Pi, dangerous deep water is over the earth; in
Ts'ui, the water has gathered together into a pool,
fulfilling the search for unity represented in Pi.

THE JUDGMENT
Congregation brings success. The king makes his way
to the temple of his ancestors, and it is favourable to
see the great man: progress and success. Righteous
persistence brings its reward. Important sacrifices are
made, bringing good fortune. It is favourable to have
a destination in view.

COMMENTARY
Ts'ui symbolises congregation, assembling together,
union. The trigram K'un, representing willing
acceptance, is joined with Tui, meaning joy. A strong
yang line occupies the fifth position, the place of
the ruler; hence the meaning of union. The king
makes his way to the ancestral temple to make his
offerings to the spirits of his forbears and so secure
the prosperity of his people. Congregation is implied
in the meeting with a great man, and persistence is
necessary for the purpose of putting matters to right.
Sacrifices must be made in accordance with the rules
of heaven; and by observing the way in which all
things congregate, we learn to understand the inner
nature of everything in earth and in heaven.

THE IMAGE
Above the earth, a pool of water gathering: the
image of Ts'ui. The superior man, accordingly,
makes ready his weapons, forearmed against the
unlooked for.

THE LINES
In the bottom line, SIX signifies:
*Sincerity, but without pertinacity, brings sometimes
disorder, at times union. He cried out and a grasping
hand made him laugh again. No regrets; go forward
without blame.*
The group cannot agree who is to be its leader. But if
they recognise their dilemma, reassurance from their
prospective leader will unite them.

In the second line, SIX signifies:
*Let yourself be drawn forward, assuring good fortune and no
blame. If you are sincere, even a small sacrifice is acceptable.*
There are subliminal forces that bring men together,
and by accepting these, we profit.

In the third line, SIX signifies:
*The congregation is sad, for no destination seems
favourable. Yet going forward brings no blame, only a
little regret.*
If a man discovers that the group he hoped to join
lacks direction, it is better that he advances alone,
even though he may suffer some pain.

In the fourth line, NINE signifies:
Great good fortune. No blame.
The fourth line, the place of the minister – he gathers
people around him in the service of his prince.

In the fifth line, NINE signifies:
*In his high position he gathers people together. No blame.
If some have no confidence in him, let him persevere in
virtue and dispose of all regrets.*
If people support a man solely because of his status, he
must gain their confidence by devotion to duty.

In the sixth line, SIX signifies:
Sighing and weeping. But no blame.
If the good intentions of a man are misunderstood,
he will be sad. But he is not to be blamed.

46. 升 Sheng
Moving Upwards

THE TRIGRAMS
ABOVE: K'un Earth, the passive
BELOW: Sun wind, gentleness, penetration
The lower trigram. Sun, also symbolises wood.
This hexagram represents (rather like hexagram
3, Chun) the action of a shoot in the earth
pushing upward with effort.

THE JUDGMENT
Moving upwards with effort against restraint
brings success. Seek out the great man and have
no fears. There is advantage to the south.

COMMENTARY
The weak line moves upwards at the proper
time. In this hexagram, gentleness and willing
acceptance are joined together. The strong line
in the central position of the lower trigram wins
response from the upper trigram, indicating great
progress and success. Unexpected good fortune
will result from the desire to see the great man
and the concomitant freedom from fear or anxiety
that will result. Southward lies the way to fortune,
and all desires will eventually be fulfilled.

THE IMAGE
Wood growing upwards in the earth: The image
of Sheng. The superior man, in accordance with
this, pays careful attention to his virtue, and
accumulates the small developments of it, till it is
high and great.

THE LINES

In the bottom line, SIX signifies:
Move upward, welcomed by those above.
Great good fortune.
The beginning of a rise from obscurity to
power enabled by those in higher positions.

In the second line, NINE signifies:
Sincere, though he made only a small sacrifice
He suffers no blame.
A man of strong character will not be criticised
even if he is out of tune with his surroundings.

In the third line, NINE signifies:
He moves upward into an unoccupied city.
The man of ambition ascends unimpeded, like a
liberator entering a city that has been abandoned.

In the fourth line, SIX signifies:
The king makes offerings on Mount Ch'i: Good fortune
and no blame.
Prince Chou, son of King Wen, provided the texts
for the individual lines. Wen made sacrifices at the
shrine on Mount Ch'i and honoured his assistants.

In the fifth line, SIX signifies:
Righteous persistence brings good fortune but one moves
upward step by step.
A man must go steadily onwards, patiently making
his way, overlooking nothing.

In the sixth line, SIX signifies:
Moving upward in darkness. Unremitting persistence
is favourable.
Blind ambition can lead one to failure. Know
what one means to do: the outcome may still be
material loss, but some advantage will be gained.

47. 困 K'un
Exhaustion

THE TRIGRAMS
ABOVE: Tui a pool of water, joy
BELOW: K'an water, dangerous pit
K'un represents a pool which has drained away into the deep pit; the water in the pool is exhausted. Within the joyousness of Tui, there is an abyss.

THE JUDGMENT
Though there is exhaustion and adversity, righteous persistence will lead to eventual success. There is good fortune for the truly great man, and no blame. Even though he has something to say, however, his words will not be heeded.

COMMENTARY
Joy and danger are joined together: adversity comes from something that lies hidden. He who succeeds in spite of the difficulties that face him is certainly one of the truly great; the strong line in the fifth place indicates that righteous persistence will bring good fortune to such a man. But since his words will not be heeded, it is most sensible for him not to speak at all.

THE IMAGE
The water of the pool has drained away; the image of K'un. The superior man will even risk his life to achieve the result that he wishes.

THE LINES
In the bottom line, SIX signifies:
Exhausted by the bare branches that entangle him, he strays into a gloomy valley and for three years meets no-one.
Until a man can begin to think constructively about his situation, there will be no way out for him.

In the second line, NINE signifies:
Exhausted, even with a meal before him. A minister in his scarlet sash arrives; now is the moment to make sacrifice. Going forward brings misfortune, but no blame.
The minister is a messenger from the prince, who is seeking able men. Nevertheless, the time is not yet ripe for setting out; first everything must be prepared.

In the third line, SIX signifies:
Exhausted by the rocks that face him, he finds nothing to lean on but thistles and briars. Returning to his house, he finds his wife has gone. Misfortune.
A man too easily discouraged by adversity. Turning back from the obstruction to seek rest at home, he finds that even there he can depend on nothing.

In the fourth line, NINE signifies:
He advances very slowly, delayed by the golden carriage in front. There are regrets, but not for long.
A newly wealthy man finds the ways of the rich an obstruction to his spiritual growth. However, his underlying strength will overcome these drawbacks.

In the fifth line, NINE signifies:
His nose and feet are cut off; oppression at the hands of the scarlet-sashed minister. Slowly, however, joy comes to him. Now is the time for sacrifice.
The man is obstructed both above and below and receives no assistance from those whose duty it should be to help. But, in time, matters will improve.

In the sixth line, SIX signifies.
Exhausted by the clinging creepers, tottering on the edge of a cliff, he tells himself 'If I move I shall regret it.' But repenting former mistakes, he can go forward to good fortune.
The difficulties are slight but the man is indecisive. If he makes up his mind, recognising his errors, all will be well.

48. 井 K'un
The Well

THE TRIGRAMS
ABOVE: K'an water, dangerous pit
BELOW: Sun wind, gentleness, penetration
The trigram Sun is also associated with wood, and this hexagram, with water above and wood below, represents the well – perhaps lined with wooden boards – in which the water is lifted up in clay or wooden pitchers attached to wooden poles.

THE JUDGMENT
In Ching, we are reminded that though the place of a town may be moved, the places of its wells cannot be changed. A well neither increases nor decreases; people come and go and draw water to their satisfaction. But sometimes, just when one is almost down to the water, the rope is not quite long enough, or the pitcher breaks – misfortune.

COMMENTARY
It is the combination of wood with water, the wood raising the water up, that gives the symbolism of the well. It is the strong yang line in the centre of the upper trigram that implies the unmoving nature of the well and its unchanging contents. The shortness of the rope indicates that we may fail to achieve what appears to be within our grasp; the breaking of the pitcher warns of certain misfortune.

THE IMAGE
Water above wood, the image of Ching. The superior man encourages people as they work, advising them how they may best help one another.

THE LINES
In the bottom line, SIX signifies:
When the well is muddy, none drink from it;
When the well is old, no creatures come to it.
If a man lacks spiritual qualities, he is insignificant. And in the end, he will be alone.

In the second line, NINE signifies:
Fish dart in the well water
The pitcher is broken and leaks.
A man who possesses good qualities that he makes no use of; he associates with inferiors and deteriorates.

In the third line, NINE signifies:
The well is cleansed, but still, to my heart's sorrow, no-one comes to drink from it. Yet the water could be drawn. If the king were wise, many could share his good fortune.
A capable man is at hand, but his abilities are not recognised.

In the fourth line, SIX signifies:
The well is being lined. No error.
Sometimes one must devote one's energies to one's own spiritual improvement, and at this time it is impossible to help others.

In the fifth line, NINE signifies:
The well water is cool from an icy spring and all may drink.
A virtuous man in a position of authority is an example to everyone.

In the sixth line, SIX signifies:
The well is uncovered, all may draw without hindrance. Have confidence. Great good fortune.
The really great man is like a dependable well, forbidden to none; and the more people take from him, the greater his spiritual wealth.

Throwing Off

THE TRIGRAMS
ABOVE: Tui a pool of water, joy
BELOW: Li fire, brightness, beauty

In its original sense, Ko means an animal's pelt that moults or its skin that is shed every year. By extension, it can be taken to mean a great political change or revolution, retaining the original sense of 'revolution', a turn of the wheel of time or fate. The two trigrams making up the hexagram are the same as in K'uei (hexagram 38, Opposites), but are reversed, the younger daughter being above and the elder below, so that the opposites are in direct conflict like water over fire.

THE JUDGMENT
When there is revolution, none will believe in it before the day of its completion, but then there is complete success. Righteous persistence brings reward, regrets vanish.

COMMENTARY
Water and fire extinguish each other, like two women who share the same household but whose wills are in constant conflict. The revolution must come first, before the faith of the people in it will be established. An enlightened attitude, both to the change itself and to the means by which it is brought about, will bring joy in success, making it possible to put everything to rights. It is the power of the forces of heaven and earth to bring about the renewal that is revealed in the progress of the four seasons. Tang and Wu (Ch'eng T'ang, 'the completer', the first of the Shang emperors, and Wu Wang, the son of King Wen) revolted in accordance with the will of heaven, and the people answered their call. Great indeed are the events of the time of throwing off.

THE IMAGE
Fire below water, the image of Ko. The superior man makes observations of the calendar, and determines the days and seasons.

THE LINES
In the bottom line, NINE signifies:
He is wrapped in the skin of a yellow ox.
The ox is the symbol of docility, yellow is the colour of the middle way. The wise man will not make changes until the time is ripe.

In the second line, SIX signifies:
When the day comes, throw off. Go forward with good fortune. No blame.
One should always attempt first to secure reform by moderate means, but when these are unsuccessful, revolution becomes necessary.

In the third line, NINE signifies:
Action brings misfortune. Persistence brings danger. But when throwing off has been three times discussed, one may commit oneself and be believed.
This is a warning against haste and ruthlessness in initiating change, as well as against delay in the name of righteousness.

In the fourth line, NINE signifies:
Regrets vanish. One is accepted by the people. Throwing off brings good fortune.
He who brings about a revolution of any kind must have the authority to maintain supporters.

In the fifth line, NINE signifies:
The great man makes his changes as the tiger moults his pelt. Even before he consults the oracle, he is believed.
The tiger moults but its stripes, although different, remain clear. When a great man leads a revolution, the reasons for his changes are apparent to all.

In the sixth line, SIX signifies:
The superior man makes his changes as the leopard moults his pelt. The inferior man changes his face. Beginning brings misfortune. Righteous persistence brings good fortune.
The leopard's moult makes only small changes in its spotted coat. After the revolution, the superior man makes small, not radical, changes to the new order.

50. 鼎 Ting
The Cauldron

THE TRIGRAMS
ABOVE: Li fire, brightness, beauty
BELOW: Sun wind, gentleness, penetration
The hexagram is the image of a cauldron: at the bottom are the legs, above them the rounded belly, then the handles like ears, and at the top the rim. The cauldron is the symbol of the nourishment it contains, and it is also the sacrificial vessel. It stands in the fire, fanned by the wind.

THE JUDGMENT
Great good fortune and success.

COMMENTARY
The cauldron represents the peace and beauty indicated by its two component trigrams, just as wood (represented by Sun) and fire combine to cook the sacrificial offering. The sages cooked their sacrifices in order to make them more acceptable to the supreme being, and made lavish feasts to nourish their wise and capable helpers. Ting is the symbol of flexible obedience: ears are made quick of hearing, and eyesight is sharpened. The weak yin line enters and ascends to the fifth place, where it responds to the strong yang lines below. All these things indicate great progress and success.

THE IMAGE
Fire upon wood, the image of Ting. The superior man, assuming a righteous posture, holds firmly to the decrees of heaven.

THE LINES
In the bottom line, SIX signifies:
The cauldron is turned over to empty it of decaying meat. Taking a concubine to bear sons, brings no blame.
Reversing the normal order of things is acceptable when the reason for the action is good.

In the second line, NINE signifies:
The cauldron is filled and my friends are envious. But they cannot harm me. Good fortune.
The man who has obtained some achievement will be the envy of everyone, but he is unassailable.

In the third line, NINE signifies:
The handles of the cauldron are broken. It cannot be moved. The fat pheasant goes uneaten. When sudden rains come, regret fades away and good fortune comes in the end.
A man whose abilities are unrecognised – a cauldron too hot too touch – is rendered ineffectual. But the rainstorm, which cools the fire, is a good omen.

In the fourth line, NINE signifies:
The legs of the cauldron are broken. The prince's dinner is spilled and his garments splashed. Misfortune.
A careless man brings misfortune not only upon himself but on his superiors.

In the fifth line, SIX signifies:
The cauldron has yellow handles and a golden rim. Righteous persistence brings its reward.
The problems in the previous two texts have been resolved. The man in authority is approachable and finds competent helpers.

In the sixth line, NINE signifies:
The cauldron has a rim of jade – great good fortune. Everything is favourable.
In the preceding text, the rim of gold denotes strength and purity; jade is hard, but also lustrous. The sage gives good advice to everyone.

51. 震 Chen
Thunderclap

THE TRIGRAMS
ABOVE: Chen thunder and awakening
BELOW: Chen thunder and awakening
The trigram Chen, repeated here, represents
the eldest son, one who is likely to take over the
leadership. Twice a strong yang line develops below
two yin lines, its energy pushing it forcibly upwards.
Like thunder, which bursts out with a terrifying clap,
the movement produces surprise and terror.

THE JUDGMENT
Chen portends success. First comes the shock, evoking
apprehension and fear, then the aftermath of laughter.
For a hundred miles around people are terrified, but
the sincere worshipper does not let his sacrifical cup
and spoon drop.

COMMENTARY
Thunder indicates success: but the initial terror is
followed by happiness. The thunder itself is like what
it provokes: shouts and laughter, fearful glee. Those
who are a hundred miles away are startled, and those
who are close at hand are terrified. Nevertheless,
someone makes his appearance who can guard the
ancestral temple and the shrines of the rural gods, one
who is fit to preside at the sacrifical ceremonies.

THE IMAGE
Thunder repeated is the image of Chen. The
superior man, in fear and trembling, develops his
virtues and examines his faults.

THE LINES
In the bottom line, NINE signifies:
*The thunderclap comes: oh! oh! Laughter and cheer
follow. Good fortune.*
First comes the shock, but afterwards there is relief.

In the second line, SIX signifies:
*Thunder comes closer. Danger is at hand. He loses every
one of his possessions and flees into the nine hills. He
should not go in search of them for after seven days he
will recover them.*
In danger, the only course is to retreat to safety.
Within a reasonable time all will be well again.

In the third line, SIX signifies:
*Thunder is everywhere, driving one to distraction.
Acting impetuously now will bring no misfortune.*
This time it is wise to act upon the spur of the
moment. It may bring little good, but will do no harm.

In the fourth line, NINE signifies:
After the thunderclap, the ways are deep in mud.
The shock has produced dazed confusion. There is
little to do but wait for conditions to improve.

In the fifth line, SIX signifies:
*Thunder rolls about the heavens, danger is at hand.
With care, nothing is lost, but there are matters
for attention.*
By holding firm at the centre of the disturbance,
one avoids loss and may achieve something.

In the sixth line, SIX signifies:
*Thunder brings chaos, people gaze around in terror.
Taking action brings misfortune, for though we are not
ourselves touched, our neighbours are harmed. No blame.
Although our nearest speak against us.*
The man who keeps his head clear amidst fear and
chaos will be able to rise above slander.

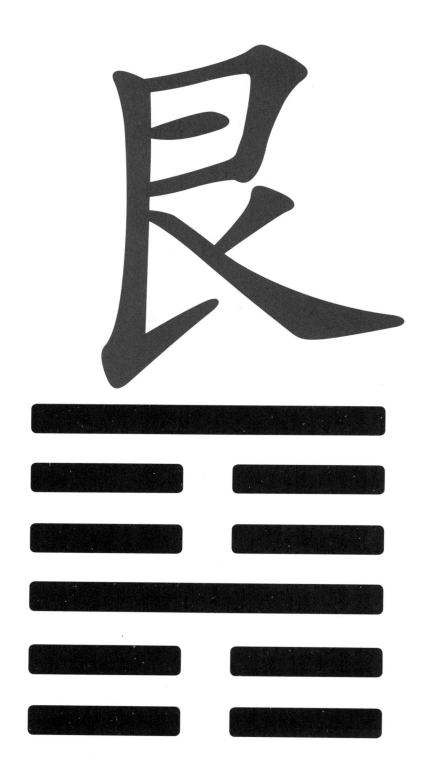

52. 艮 Ken

Inaction

THE TRIGRAMS
ABOVE: Ken mountain, stillness
BELOW: Ken mountain, stillness
In this hexagram the male principle, represented by the yang lines, is striving upwards, and the female principle, represented by the yin lines, moves downwards. The inaction results from the fact that these movements have come to a conclusion in each trigram.

THE JUDGMENT
Keeping the back unmoving so that one no longer feels one's body; walking out into the courtyard without noticing the people there – there is no blame. [In Taoism, the spine is thought of as a sort of still connecting three 'crucibles': one at the base of the spine, one at the level of the solar plexus behind the stomach, and the third in the head.]

COMMENTARY
Ken signifies resting, desisting, coming to a stop. When it is the time for inaction, that is the time to stop; when the time comes for action, then act! By action and inaction, each at its appointed time, man makes glorious progress. The inaction represented by Ken means inaction in its proper place and time. The upper and the lower trigrams exactly correspond to each other, but do not interact; hence the wording of the Judgment.

THE IMAGE
The mountains stand together, the image of Ken. The superior man, accordingly, does not move in his thoughts beyond the position in which he finds himself.

THE LINES
In the bottom line, SIX signifies:
His toes are still. No blame.
The toes represent the simplest sort of movement. A man who knows the importance of inaction at the beginning will find the right way.

In the second line, SIX signifies:
His calves are still. He cannot aid the one he follows and is disquieted.
The legs have begun a movement, but it is suddenly halted. The course he was pursuing was wrong.

In the third line, NINE signifies:
His loins are still, his spine is stiff. Danger. The heart is suffocated.
He who endeavours to stifle sexual desire when his mind is not prepared for it will suffer painful results.

In the fourth line, SIX signifies:
His trunk is still. No blame.
A policy of inaction at this time is appropriate, even though the initiate is not yet free of his doubts.

In the fifth line, SIX signifies:
His jaws are still. His speech being ordered, he has no cause for regret.
To know when to speak and when not to speak is the way to true wisdom.

In the sixth line, NINE signifies:
He is noble in his inaction. Good fortune.
This is the goal of inaction: spiritual nobility, which brings nothing but good fortune in its train.

Gradual Progress

THE TRIGRAMS
ABOVE: Sun wind, gentleness
BELOW: Ken mountain, stillness
In this hexagram Sun also represents wood, just as a tree on a mountain, caressed by the wind, grows slowly according to the laws of nature.

THE JUDGMENT
The maiden is given in marriage, bringing good fortune. Righteous perseverance is advantageous.

COMMENTARY
The gradual progress symbolised by Chien is like the marriage of a young woman; there is good fortune for herself and for the man she marries, and in the dowry that she brings with her. The lines move upwards, each in its correct place, to the strong yang line in the fifth position, the position of the ruler. Gradually progressing in righteousness, a man becomes fit to rule his land. The unmoving quality of the mountain, conjoined with the gentleness of the wind, gives rise to inexhaustible activity.

THE IMAGE
Upon the mountain stands a tree, the symbol of gradual progress. The superior man, accordingly, abides in dignity and virtue, inclining the people to good behaviour.

THE LINES
In the bottom line, SIX signifies:
The wild geese gradually approach the shore. The younger son is in danger, and spoken against. But there is no blame.
The wild goose (the symbol of marital fidelity because it was believed it only took one mate in life) flies towards the sun (the male principle), like a young woman seeking a husband. A young man embarking on life is sensitive to criticism, but he is not the cause of any of his troubles.

In the second line, SIX signifies:
The wild geese gradually approach the cliff. They eat and drink in peace and joy. Good fortune.
In terms of marriage, this represents material success.

In the third line, NINE signifies:
The wild geese gradually approach the dry plains. The husband goes forth and does not return. The wife is with child but does not give birth. Misfortune.
The dry plains are no safe place for geese. The marriage is unsuccessful; the husband endangers his family.

In the fourth line, SIX signifies:
The wild geese gradually approach the trees. Perhaps they will find a branch to perch. No blame.
Trees, also, are unsuitable places for geese, but they may provide some refuge. In marriage, one partner may bring stability by thoughtful acts.

In the fifth line, NINE signifies:
The wild geese gradually approach the high ground. For three years the wife is without child but in the end all will be well. Good fortune.
In a high position a man can become isolated from his family or colleagues. But as progress continues, misunderstandings will be cleared away.

In the sixth line, NINE signifies:
The wild geese gradually approach the summits. Their feathers are used in sacred rites. Good fortune.
The superior man rises far beyond the reach of ordinary mortals, but still his blessings fall like goose feathers.

The Marriageable Maiden

THE TRIGRAMS
ABOVE: Chen thunder and awakening
BELOW: Tui a pool of water, joy
Chen represents the eldest son and Tui the youngest daughter. The hexagram represents the older man leading a young girl through the door of his house. But the girl is not his first wife; she is his second wife or perhaps the first of his concubines. For this reason Kuei Mei is not a very fortunate omen, even though it should not be taken as referring in every case to marriage.

THE JUDGMENT
Kuei Mei is the marriageable maiden. Going forward brings misfortune, and no destination is at present favourable.

COMMENTARY
This hexagram symbolishes the proper relationship between heaven and earth; for if heaven and earth had no intercourse, nothing would come into existence and flourish. The marriage of the younger sister is both her end and her beginning. Joy and movement together (represented by the two trigrams) – this is the image of a maiden marrying. But the inappropriate positions of the third and fifth lines indicate that going forward will bring misfortune, for the weak yin lines are mounted upon the strong yang lines.

THE IMAGE
Thunder over the water, the image of Kuei Mei. The superior man, accordingly, understands the mischief that may be made at the beginning in order to reach a lasting conclusion.

THE LINES
In the bottom line, NINE signifies:
The maiden marries as a concubine. The lame man can still walk. Going forward brings good fortune.
The girl who enters a family in the position of first concubine has no power of her own, but can still advance herself.

In the second line, NINE signifies:
The one-eyed man can still see. The hermit can still advance himself by righteous perseverance.
A man who neglects the affections of his concubine is like a man with one eye: he is concerned only with his own interests.

In the third line, SIX signifies:
The maiden was but a slave and rose to become a concubine.
Desperate to improve one's position, one can take the first opportunity offered, however small.

In the fourth line, NINE signifies:
The maiden remains unwed beyond the proper day. But a late marriage comes in time.
A girl may delay her marriage, in the good expectation of finding the right husband even until it seems too late.

In the fifth line, SIX signifies:
The Emperor I gave his daughter in marriage. Her garments were not as fine as those of her bridesmaid. The moon is near full and brings good fortune.
T'ang the Completer decreed that his daughters, though of highest rank, should be subordinate to their husbands. Similarly, shortly before it is full, the moon shines brightly but does not yet directly oppose the sun.

In the sixth line, SIX signifies:
The woman holds the basket, but there is nothing in it. The man sacrifices the sheep, but no blood flows. Having no destination is favourable.
The empty basket and bloodless sheep signify ritual without sincerity. There is no advantage in proceeding.

55. 豐 Feng
Abundance

THE TRIGRAMS
ABOVE: Chen thunder and awakening
BELOW: Li fire, brightness
Chen, symbolising movement, is above Li, symbolising clarity: this combination produces abundance. However, here the height of development has been reached, suggesting that such a situation will not endure indefinitely.

THE JUDGMENT
Abundance means great success: the greatness of the king is an inspiration. Do not be downhearted, for the bright sun is now at its zenith.

COMMENTARY
Brilliance conjoined with movement signifies abundance. The king has still greater possibilities before him: he inspires his people and they respect him, he shines like a sun before the whole world. But the sun at its zenith begins to decline; the moon that has waxed begins to wane. So all that is in heaven and earth grows and diminishes according to the season; and how much truer indeed is this of men, as well as of the gods.

THE IMAGE
Thunder and lightning come together, the image of Feng. The superior man, accordingly, hears law suits, judges and inflicts the necessary penalties.

THE LINES
In the bottom line, NINE signifies:
Meeting his equal, accepting his hospitality for ten days, there is no error. Going forward earns respect.
Those who represent the attributes of brilliance and movement are well matched. Nevertheless, the time comes when it is essential to go forward again.

In the second line, SIX signifies:
The shadows close in. The polestar can be seen at noonday. Going forward now invites mistrust and hate. But sincere devotion brings good fortune.
When the machinations of a powerful party obscure the brilliance of the ruler, the wise man gives up any ideas of energetic advance.

In the third line, NINE signifies:
The shadows are thick as a great banner and at noonday the smallest stars are visible. Though he break his right arm, there is no blame.
All is now in eclipse. Even the right-hand man of the ruler has no power to undertake anything.

In the fourth line, NINE signifies:
The shadows are like a huge tent, the polestar can be seen at noonday. He meets his prince, an equal. Good fortune
The eclipse is beginning to pass. Meeting with a prince of equal rank indicates that the time for action is almost arrived.

In the fifth line, SIX signifies:
Light begins to appear in the sky as after a storm. Unexpected good fortune and fame draw near.
The dominance of the adversary's party is waning, and the ruler's wise men propose modest action.

In the sixth line, SIX signifies:
His house is full of abundance nd there is a wall about it. Peeping out through the gate, he sees no-one. For three years – nobody. Misfortune.
In devoting his attentions solely to material success he has cut himself off from everybody.

56. 旅 Lü
The Wayfarer

THE TRIGRAMS
ABOVE: Li fire, brightness
BELOW: Ken mountain, stillness
The mountain, Ken, is unmoving; while the fire, Li, burns upward. The two trigrams have nothing to hold them together, and so represent the separation that is the fate of the wayfarer.

THE JUDGMENT
Lü, the wayfarer, signifies success in small matters. Perseverance brings good fortune to the travelling man.

COMMENTARY
The weak yin line in the centre of the upper trigram is freely subservient to the yang lines on either side of it. The obstinacy represented by the mountain, conjoined to the beauty of fire, indicates success in small matters, and the good fortune that will eventually come to determined wayfarers. Great is the time and great the right course indicated by Lü.

THE IMAGE
Fire upon the mountain is the image of Lü. The superior man, accordingly, is wise and cautious in imposing penalties, and does not allow lawsuits to drag on.

THE LINES
In the bottom line, SIX signifies:
The wayfarer concerns himself with trifles and so attracts calamity.
The traveller is humble and defenceless, and so should preserve his spiritual dignity, and avoid the disputes he finds along the road.

In the second line, SIX signifies:
The wayfarer reaches an inn, his valuables safe in his bosom, and finds a young servant loyal to him.
In preserving his spiritual dignity, the traveller wins the allegiance of a trustworthy follower.

In the third line, NINE signifies:
Careless, he burns down the inn, and loses his loyal servant. Though firm and correct, he is in danger.
Through his own irresponsibility, the traveller loses everything. Whatever his plans, it would be folly to attempt to proceed with them at this moment.

In the fourth line, NINE signifies:
The wayfarer finds a roadside shelter, he earns his living and acquires an axe. But still he laments that his heart is not glad.
The traveller restricts his ambition to what he can immediately achieve. He makes a living but has not found a home.

In the fifth line, SIX signifies:
He shoots at a pheasant but loses his arrow. However, in the end, he wins praise and gains high office.
The wayfarer tries to shoot a pheasant to impress a prince. Although he is unsuccessful in this, he eventually receives great benefits.

In the sixth line, NINE signifies:
The bird burns its own nest. As first the wayfarer laughs and then he cries and weeps. Careless, he loses his cow. Misfortune.
The bird burning its own nest is the phoenix, a symbol of high virtue, but there is a suggestion that carelessness is responsible for the burnt nest.

57. 巽 Sun
Submission

THE TRIGRAMS
ABOVE: Sun wind, gentleness
BELOW: Sun wind, gentleness
This is one of the eight double trigrams; Sun represents the eldest daughter and gentleness, but like the wind – or like wood, with which it is also identified – it has the property of penetration. In the natural world, the wind penetrates the clouds, bringing clarity and serenity; in human affairs, it is the penetrating clarity of intelligence that uncovers the darkness of intrigue and perversity.

THE JUDGMENT
Submission and gentleness lead to success in many minor matters. It is advantageous to have a destination in view and to visit a great man.

COMMENTARY
Willing submission is necessary in carrying out the will of heaven. The strong yang line is correctly in the fifth place, indicating that what is willed will be fulfilled. The weak yin lines in first and fourth place are both obedient to the yang lines above them, indicating moderate success, and the advantage of movement in any direction.

THE IMAGE
Winds follow one upon the other the image of Sun. The superior man, accordingly. makes his commands known once more, and performs his tasks according to the will of heaven.

THE LINES
In the bottom line, SIX signifies:
Coming and going like the wind. He should seek advantage in righteous persistence like a brave soldier.
Indecisiveness is the outcome of submissiveness. Behaving with the persistance of a military commander can bring advance.

In the second line, NINE signifies:
He creeps beneath the bed. And consults a confusion of magicians and diviners. But there is good fortune and no error.
When motives are hidden and their outcome cannot be decided, it is not blameworthy to make use of any means in determining what is to come.

In the third line, NINE signifies:
He penetrates repeatedly and must give way. Humiliation.
It is better to reach a decision quickly than to come eventually to an impasse as a result of constant questioning.

In the fourth line, SIX signifies:
The time for regret is past. Three kinds of game are found in the hunt.
When one occupies an important administrative position in which experience, innate modesty and decisive action can be combined, success is assured.

In the fifth line, NINE signifies:
Righteous persistence brings good fortune. Regrets vanish, and everything is favourable. There is no good beginning but a good end. Three days before the change and three days after bring good fortune.
The beginning may not have been propitious, but almost unexpectedly the right time will make itself apparent.

In the sixth line, NINE signifies:
He creeps beneath the bed. He loses his living and his axe. Persistence brings misfortune.
The subject of this text is too submissive, showing humility amounting to servility.

58. 兌 Tui

Joy

THE TRIGRAMS
ABOVE: Tui a pool of water, joy
BELOW: Tui a pool of water, joy
This hexagram is another of the eight which are made up of doubled trigrams. Tui is the youngest daughter, whose gentleness brings joy through the strength of the strong yang lines in the fourth and fifth place.

THE JUDGMENT
Joy means success. Righteous perseverance brings its just reward.

COMMENTARY
Tui signifies satisfaction in gladness. In each of the trigrams there is a strong yang line in the centre, with a weak yin line above it. This shows that seeking joy through righteous persistence is the right way to accord with the will of heaven and to reach concordance with the feelings of one's fellow men. When the people are led with gladness, they forget their burdens; as they wrestle in joy with their difficulties, they even forget that they must die. The great power of joy lies in the encouragement that it can give to all.

THE IMAGE
The waters resting one upon the other, the image of joy. The superior man, accordingly, joins with his friends in discussion and practises with them.

THE LINES
In the bottom line, NINE signifies:
Contented joy. Good fortune.
The quiet strength that contented joy confers: wordless, self-contained and free from all envy.

In the second line, NINE signifies:
Sincere joy. Good fortune, No regrets.
The sincerely joyous man will not be distracted by doubtful pleasures offered by inferiors.

In the third line, SIX signifies:
Coming joy. Misfortune.
There is disagreement about this text. It seems probable that it means that misfortune is experienced when a happy event is expected.

In the fourth line, NINE signifies:
Calculating joys to come, he is restless. Close to misfortune, he nevertheless is happy.
If a man is aware of the danger of indulgence and makes his decision accordingly, he will experience true joy.

In the fifth line, NINE signifies:
Putting one's trust in crumbling things, means danger.
It is important to be very much on one's guard, so as to be able to draw back when the first signs of disintegration become apparent.

In the sixth line, SIX signifies:
Joy in seduction.
He has abandoned his spiritual advancement to give himself over to the joys of the flesh and of material things.

59. 渙 Huan
Dispersal

THE TRIGRAMS
ABOVE: Sun wind, gentleness
BELOW: K'an water, dangerous pit
The wind blows across the water, dispersing it
into spume, mists, and eventually drying it up. So
a man's energy, dammed up within him, may be
released by gentleness.

THE JUDGMENT
Huan indicates progress and success. The
king approaches his ancestral temple; and it is
advantageous to cross the great water, and to be
righteously persistent in all.

COMMENTARY
Successful progress is symbolised by the strong
yang line in the second place, which is not
exhausted there. The weak yin line in fourth
place is outside the lower trigram, and the fifth
line above – representing the king – responds to
it. The king approaching his ancestral temple,
and occupying the centre of the upper trigram,
is maintaining his position without any change of
mind. One of the additional attributes of Sun is
wood; the advantage of crossing the great water
derives from mounting on a vessel of wood, and
great success is the result.

THE IMAGE
The wind blows over the water, the image of Huan.
So the kings of old built temples in which to
sacrifice to the supreme being.

THE LINES
In the bottom line, SIX signifies:
He brings assistance with the strength of a horse.
Good fortune.
The wind over the water can bring clouds, which,
if not dispersed, will bring rain. Join together in
action before divisions of opinion arise.

In the second line, NINE signifies:
In the midst of dispersal, he hastens to the altar.
Regrets vanish.
One should find some spiritual means of
protection from evil.

In the third line, SIX signifies:
All self-interest is dispersed. No regrets.
Only by a great renunciation can a man obtain the
strength to achieve great things.

In the fourth line, SIX signifies
He disperses his followers. Great good fortune.
Dispersal leads to accumulation, good men standing
like a mound. Something that ordinary people would
not have thought of.
Ridding himself of incompetent companions,
the well intentioned man will soon be joined by
virtuous followers.

In the fifth line, NINE signifies:
He issues his proclamations as sweat flows from the body.
The king scatters his stores among the people
without blame.
Just as a high fever is dispersed in perspiration, so
the king may relieve his anxieties by dispersing his
possessions among the needy.

In the sixth line, NINE signifies:
He disperses bloodiness, keeping evil at a distance.
Departing without blame.
There is disagreement upon this text, but it seems
that 'dispersing bloodiness' means avoiding
bloodshed and removing oneself from danger.

60. 節 Chieh
Restraint

THE TRIGRAMS
ABOVE: K'an dangerous deep water
BELOW: Tui a pool of water, joy
The word Chieh really means the joints of bamboo, or the joints of the human frame, or the natural divisions of the year. Thus it represents the voluntary limitations that may be set upon growth or expenditure. The pool of water can only occupy a limited space. The movement of more water from above must be restrained or the pool will overflow.

THE JUDGMENT
Restraint brings success and progress. But restrictions that are severe and difficult should not be perpetuated.

COMMENTARY
Chieh signifies success because the strong yang lines and the weak yin lines are equal in number, and there is a yang line in fifth position. Severe and difficult restrictions should not be allowed to continue because they produce exhaustion. Even in the midst of danger we experience pleasure and satisfaction in following the proper course. It is by the restraint exercised between terrestrial and celestial forces that the four seasons arrive each at its appointed time; so, when due restraint is shown in the duties of government, the state suffers no injury, and the people no hurt.

THE IMAGE
Water above the pool, the image of Chieh. The superior man, accordingly, creates his system of number and measure, and discusses the nature of virtue and proper conduct.

THE LINES
In the bottom line, NINE signifies:
He restricts himself to the outer gates and courtyard.
No blame.
The man who knows how to limit himself against insuperable obstacles can accumulate an energy that will enable him to act positively.

In the second line, NINE signifies:
He restricts himself to the courtyard within his gate.
Misfortune.
When the time for action arrives, it is essential to act at once.

In the third line, SIX signifies:
He places no restraint upon himself: lamentations
But no blame.
Those who give themselves up to indulgence may regret it, but if they accept responsibility they are not to be condemned.

In the fourth line, SIX signifies:
He restrains himself contentedly. Success.
Effective self-limitation.

In the fifth line, NINE signifies:
He restrains himself sweetly and voluntarily.
Good fortune. Going forward brings approbation.
When an important man restricts his own actions and does not demand too much from his associates, it will be met with general approval.

In the sixth line, SIX signifies:
Troublesome restraint. Persistence brings misfortune
But there is no regret.
Restrictions that are too severe will not be endured for long. Nevertheless, occasionally a certain ruthlessness on oneself is the only way to salvation.

61. 中孚 Chung Fu
Inner Truth

THE TRIGRAMS
ABOVE: Sun wind, gentleness, penetration
BELOW: Tui a pool of water, joy
The wind blows over the water, revealing its invisible movement in visible disturbance of the surface. The strong yang lines above and below, and the yielding yin lines in the centre, indicate a heart free from prejudice and open to the truth. At the same time, the strong line at the centre of each trigram indicates the strength of inner truth.

THE JUDGMENT
Inner truth and sincerity: the pig with the fish. This leads to good fortune. It is advantageous to cross the great water. Righteous persistence brings its just reward.

COMMENTARY
The lines reveal joy and gentleness conjoined: confidence and sincerity will ensure the development of the kingdom. The combination of the pig with the fish may be identified as the dolphin, known in all ancient mythologies as a friendly guide on a journey, and as one who can save a sailor from drowning: so good fortune attends any undertaking that involves crossing the great water. Persistence accompanied by confidence is always advantageous, because it accords with the will of heaven.

THE IMAGE
Wind over the water, the image of Chung Fu. The superior man, accordingly, gives thought to matters of law and delays the sentence of death.

THE LINES
In the bottom line, NINE signifies:
Be prepared as he who fishes or hunts the boar.
Good fortune. Other intentions bring disquietude.
The angler or huntsman must be prepared but patient. An argument will only lead to anxiety.

In the second line, NINE signifies:
The crane calls in the shadows; and the young ones answer.
I have a cup of contentment and I will share it with you.
Hidden, the crane calls and its young respond. When good men hear truth, they should share it.

In the third line, SIX signifies:
He finds his equal. Now he strikes his drum, now he stops. Now he weeps, and now he sings.
The equal may be a companion or an adversary, but should one be glad that the truth has been shared or lament that others do not know it?

In the fourth line, SIX signifies:
Like the moon near its fullness, or a team-horse whose companions have broken away. No blame.
A full moon stands in opposition to the sun, but at that moment it begins to wane – we must be modest and reverent in the face of enlightenment.

In the fifth line, NINE signifies:
He seems drawn forwards by his truth and draws other with him. No error.
Only when his inner strength is sufficient can he carry others with him.

In the sixth line, NINE signifies:
Cockcrow rises to heaven.
Perseverance brings misfortune.
The cock cannot fly: only its cry rises into the skies. Overconfidence is followed by evil consequences.

62. 小過 Hsiao Kuo
The Small Persist

THE TRIGRAMS
ABOVE: Chen thunder and awakening
BELOW: Ken mountain and stillness
This hexagram represents a most unusual situation: weak yin lines enclose it on both sides, predominating, but the two strong yang lines are at the centre, creating conflict. However, it is the yin lines that must relate to the external world. A man who attains a position of authority for which he is inadequate must exercise unusual prudence.

THE JUDGMENT
The small persist. Success. Righteous perseverance brings its just reward. Small things may be accomplished, but the time is not right for great things. Birds fly high, singing, but lose their tune. It is better not to strive upwards, but to stay below.

COMMENTARY
This hexagram indicates success for the small; their persistence will be rewarded, and their deeds fit the times. The yin line in fifth place signifies success in small affairs, and good fortune. The yang line in fourth place has not succeeded in reaching a ruling position, indicating that it is not the moment for great matters. The symbol of a bird denotes that it is better to descend than to ascend; this is the way to good fortune.

THE IMAGE
Thunder upon the mountain, the image of Hsiao Kuo. The superior man, accordingly, shows excess in his reverence, too much grief in his bereavement, and too much economy in his husbandry.

THE LINES
In the bottom line, SIX signifies:
The bird flies upward and meets misfortune.
The young bird that flies too soon is courting disaster.

In the second line, SIX signifies:
Passing by the ancestor and meeting the ancestress: failing to see the prince but encountering a minister. No blame.
In the temple, to pass by the tablets of the male ancestor, going towards those of the ancestress, is unusual, but it still shows reverence and humility.

In the third line, NINE signifies:
Take unusual precautions for subordinates may come from behind to strike you. Misfortune.
The wise man is vigilant at all times.

In the fourth line, NINE signifies:
No blame. He meets him in his path and does not slip by. Going forward brings danger: be on your guard. Now is not time for action but for constant determination.
Alll opposition and obstacles in the path must be met face-on; but it is not the time for pushing forward.

In the fifth line, SIX signifies:
Dense clouds but no rain from the western marches. The prince shoots his arrow, hitting the man in the cave.
A man in authority exercises the powers that have been given to him, but in doing so he exceeds his abilities, and injures another who represents no threat to him.

In the sixth line, SIX signifies:
He passes by, not facing him. The bird flies away, meaning misfortune. Calamity and injury.
Failing to acknowledge the existence of obstacles is arrogant. Overshooting the target, one misses it.

Climax and After

THE TRIGRAMS
ABOVE: K'an dangerous deep water
BELOW: Li fire, brightness
This hexagram represents an evolutionary phase of hexagram 11 (T'ai, Peace). The strong yang lines have moved upwards into their strong positions, displacing the yin lines into their proper weak positions. Everything is in its proper place. But although this is a very favourable hexagram, it still gives grounds for caution: because it is when equilibrium has been reached that any sudden movement may cause order to revert to disorder.

THE JUDGMENT
After the climax there is success in small matters. Righteous persistence brings its reward. Good fortune in the beginning, but disorder in the end.

COMMENTARY
Chi Chi indicates progress in small matters. The proper position of the yang and yin lines shows that righteous persistence will be rewarded: the weak line at the centre of the lower trigram indicates good fortune in the beginning, but the way peters out, efforts come to an end, and disorder returns.

THE IMAGE
Water over the fire, the image of Chi Chi. The superior man, accordingly, gives due thought to the misfortunes to come, and takes precautions in advance.

THE LINES
In the bottom line, NINE signifies:
Like a driver who brakes his chariot, or a fox with a wet tail. No blame.
The wise man does not allow himself to be carried away by the general fever of enthusiasm. He is like a fox who in crossing water has only got his tail wet.

In the second line, SIX signifies:
She loses her carriage curtain. Do not run after it, for in seven days it will be recovered.
It was a breach of conduct for a woman to ride in a curtainless carriage. Someone who seeks the confidence of superiors shouldn't draw attention to themselves, but wait until their qualities are recognised.

In the third third line, NINE signifies:
The Illustrious Ancestor, the Emperor Wu Ting, attacked the country of devils. Three years he took in subduing it. Small men are not fit for such enterprises.
Around 1324BCE, Wu Ting led an expedition against barbarous tribes. Only a great man can overcome rebellions.

In the fourth line, SIX signifies:
The finest clothes turn to rags. Be careful all day long.
The wise man is not deceived by present prosperity: he is constantly on his guard against misfortune.

In the fifth line, NINE signifies:
The neighbour in the east sacrifices an ox: but it is the neighbour in the west, with his small spring sacrifice, who is blessed for his sincerity.
The western neighbour shuns ostentatious gestures but, at the right moment, makes a sincere offering and so gains good fortune.

In the sixth line, SIX signifies:
His head is in the water. Misfortune.
The man who has safely crossed water but gets his head wet, must have turned back. Going forward without looking back, one can escape misfortune.

64. 未濟 Wei Chi
Before Climax

THE TRIGRAMS
ABOVE: Li fire, brightness
BELOW: K'an dangerous deep water
This hexagram is the reverse of the previous one: the transition from disorder to order is not yet complete. Chi Chi is associated with autumn, when the year's growth is complete, but Wei Chi is associated with the burgeoning of spring.

THE JUDGMENT
Success. The little fox has almost crossed the water, but gets its tail soaked. No destination is favourable at present.

COMMENTARY
This hexagram indicates progress and success because the weak yin line in the fifth position occupies a central position in the upper trigram between the two yang lines. The little fox has crossed the stream, but he has not yet succeeded in getting past the middle of the danger. The fox's wet tail and the fact that no destination is favourable imply that there is no way at present of advancing one's affairs. Although the yin and yang lines are not in their proper places, they nevertheless accord suitably with one another.

THE IMAGE
Fire over the water, the image of Wei Chi. The superior man, accordingly, carefully distinguishes between the nature of things, and between the various places that they occupy.

THE LINES
In the bottom line, SIX signifies:
His tail is soaked: Disgrace.
In tumultuous times, there may be a temptation to push one's way forward, but such haste can lead to failure and humiliation if the time is not ripe.

In the second line, NINE signifies:
The driver brakes his chariot.
Righteous persistence brings its reward. The driver shows his persistence by applying the brake.

In the third line, SIX signifies:
The destination is not yet reached, and going forward brings misfortune. Nevertheless it is advantageous to cross the great water.
Although the time to go forward has arrived, one is not yet properly prepared. However, it is essential to preserve one's determination to advance.

In the fourth line, NINE signifies:
Righteous persistence brings good fortune. Regrets vanish. To subdue the country of the devils took great effort but after three years vast territories were won.
As in the previous hexagram, this is a reference to the campaign of Wu Ting. Only perseverance will bring success in times of struggle.

In the fifth line, SIX signifies:
Righteous persistence brings good fortune, regrets vanish. The superior man shines forth in sincerity. Success.
Victory has been won.

In the sixth place, NINE signifies:
Confident and trusted, he may drink in celebration. No blame. But if he wet his head, he loses all.
Now, at the moment of achievement before climax, is the time to celebrate. But the man who celebrates to excess will lose the trust of others.

Index to the hexagrams

Lower trigram	Upper trigram	Hexagram
		1 乾 Ch'ien
		43 夬 Kuai
		14 大有 Tayu
		34 大壯 Ta Chuang
		9 小畜 Hsiao Ch'u
		5 需 Hsü
		26 大畜 Ta Ch'u
		11 泰 T'ai

Lower trigram	Upper trigram	Hexagram
		13 同人 T'ung Jen
		49 革 Ko
		30 離 Li
		55 豐 Feng
		37 家人 Chia Jen
		63 既濟 Chi Chi
		22 賁 Pi
		36 明夷 Ming I

Lower trigram	Upper trigram	Hexagram
		10 履 Lü
		58 兌 Tui
		38 睽 K'ue
		54 歸妹 Kuei Mei
		61 中孚 Chung Fu
		60 節 Chieh
		41 損 Sun
		19 臨 Lin

Lower trigram	Upper trigram	Hexagram
		25 无妄 Wu Wang
		17 隨 Sui
		21 噬嗑 Shih Ho
		51 震 Chen
		42 益 I
		3 屯 Chun
		27 頤 I
		24 復 Fu

Lower trigram	Upper trigram	Hexagram		Lower trigram	Upper trigram	Hexagram
		44 姤 Kou				33 遯 Tun
		28 大過 Ta Kuo				31 咸 Hsien
		50 鼎 Ting				56 旅 Lü
		32 恆 Heng				62 小過 Hsiao Kuo
		57 巽 Sun				53 漸 Chien
		48 井 Ching				39 蹇 Chien
		18 蠱 Ku				52 艮 Ken
		46 升 Sheng				15 謙 Ch'ien

Lower trigram	Upper trigram	Hexagram		Lower trigram	Upper trigram	Hexagram
		6 訟 Sung				12 否 P'i
		47 困 K'un				45 萃 Ts'ui
		64 未濟 Wei Chi				35 晉 Chin
		40 解 Hsieh				16 豫 Yü
		59 渙 Huan				20 觀 Kuan
		29 坎 K'an				8 比 Pi
		4 蒙 Meng				23 剝 Po
		7 師 Shih				2 坤 K'un

Index

This edition published in 2012 by

CHARTWELL BOOKS, INC.
A division of
BOOK SALES, INC.
276 Fifth Avenue Suite 206
New York, New York 10001
USA

Copyright © 2012 Amber Books Ltd

ISBN: 978-0-7858-2923-2

Text: Original text by Neil Powell, adapted by Kieron Connolly
Project Editor: Sarah Uttridge
Design: Rick Fawcett

Printed and bound in China

TRADITIONAL CHINESE BOOKBINDING

This book has been produced using traditional Chinese bookbinding
techniques, using a method that was developed during the Ming Dynasty
(1368–1644) and remained in use until the adoption of Western binding
techniques in the early 1900s. In traditional Chinese binding, single sheets of
paper are printed on one side only, and each sheet is folded in half, with the
printed pages on the outside. The book block is then sandwiched between
two boards and sewn together through punched holes close to the cut edges
of the folded sheets.